D1361606

THE 6 FUNCTIONS
OF MANAGEMENT

GEORGE PHIRIPPIDIS

JUN - - 2018

THE 6 FUNCTIONS OF MANAGEMENT
GEORGE PHIRIPPIDIS

Published by Kerr Hill, Inc.

2303 Camino Ramon, Suite 134, San Ramon, CA 94583

www.kerrhill.com

Cover: Aime Menendez

Design: Aime Menendez

TO CONTACT US: info@kerrhill.com

COPYRIGHTS, SERVICEMARKS AND TRADEMARKS

NOTICE OF RIGHTS

LIMIT OF LIABILITY/DISCLAIMER OF WARRANTY

ISBN 978-0-9912768-0-6

SPECIAL THANK YOU

I would like to thank my good friend Lyn
for all her inspiration, influence and direct
contribution to this book.

CONTENTS

FUNCTION ONE
COMMUNICATING   16

FUNCTION SIX
LEADING

121

"Effective leadership is
putting first things first.
Effective management is
discipling carrying it out."
- Stephen Covey

PREFACE

Welcome to The Six Functions of Management, a practical, interactive planning guide designed to help people in management positions understand, assess and create action plans for the six most critical functions of management. This guide is based on core components of a three day management course, which has been utilized by thousands of people over 22 years as a proven framework for managing oneself, their team and business.

This guide is designed to help you:

- Understand the key elements that make up each of The Six Functions of Management.

- Assess your capabilities in each function and apply tools to develop and implement personal Action Plans.

- Develop capabilities to apply the functions as needed to enhance your management role success.

The ultimate goals of this guide are to help make your management effort more efficient and effective and to provide lasting operational control, organizational alignment and benefit to your business.

AUTHOR HISTORY

Knowing about the Six Functions earlier in my career would have saved a lot of time and effort in managing not only my business, but also myself. I realize now that this framework can be applied to a variety of positions and occupations whether you are a director, project manager, mid-level or first line manager, the Six Functions are relevant to each and can be applied to your role.

In my early career, I spent 13 years selling wholesale electrical supplies to a large client base of Original Equipment Manufacturers (OEM's) in the Silicon Valley. Looking back and luckily for me, I was performing many of the Six Functions by sheer necessity of the job. However, had I known then that an actual framework existed, I could have more intentionally grown my business and the people supporting that business.

I started my second career, an e-commerce/mail order business dedicated to the development and patenting of mobile office-based products, from the ground up. If you have ever started a business from scratch you know firsthand how exciting and intense the endeavor can be. There are many moving pieces that, if not executed properly, can have sub-optimal or even disastrous results. The Six Functions would have been even more valuable to me in the different aspects of my job, such as planning and organizing for marketing, sales, operations, patenting, and to the business as a whole.

While I did well using the "Seat of the Pants" management model, the Six Functions would have focused me on leveraging my strengths and building the company with a more systematic approach.

Most people learn to manage from trial and error. When I came to Kerr Hill in 2002, I learned to use the Six Functions as a formal way to manage the business and minimize the need to rely on prior, informal management methods. I want to share what I have learned and the foundation of that learning to help you minimize "Seat of the Pants" management and equip you with the tools to see, organize and take advantage of opportunities as they come your way.

Throughout the years, I've facilitated the Six Functions program for high potential, high performance organizations of all sizes, and for managers wishing to advance to the next level. The live program typically is conducted in two and three-day sessions and has many other management tools and components as part of the workshop. Many people cannot attend these programs due to time or funding limitations, missing the opportunity to get equipped with necessary information, guidance and tools for their continued development.

I learned through my experiences that changing just one to three aspects of my management approach could yield great results. This required a willingness to embrace change. I knew something was in the process of change when I experienced two things: 1) I had to slow down and think about what I was doing instead of relying automatically on a go-to method and, 2) I felt uncomfortable with the new situation. As with most change, this discomfort would eventually dissipate as my new habits took root. I like to think of it as wearing a favorite pair of shoes. When they were new, they may not have been so comfortable to wear until they were broken in, which took repeated use. It was the same with implementing a new framework and behaviors for managing my business and personal life. I believe this planning guide can do the same for you.

GETTING STARTED

HOW TO UTILIZE THIS GUIDE

WORKBOOK HIGHLIGHTS

>> UNDERSTANDING EACH FUNCTION

>> ASSESSING YOURSELF IN EACH

>> CREATING ACTIONS PLANS TO IMPROVE

IF YOU HAVE ATTENDED other managerial trainings or read development books, you might have left with only one to three things that "stuck" with you as a result. The rest of the content may not have resonated or wasn't as applicable at the time. If you can walk away with one to three things from this planning guide that you can commit to implementing, then the experience will be well worth it. The rest of the material may become more relevant at another time.

The key components focus on the framework and tools that have worked for thousands of people over the past twenty-two years. The principles are presented in a self-paced, action-oriented design that will provide you with new insights and direction now and into the future.

This interactive guide can be approached and utilized a number of ways: 1) read it through from end to end and return to focus on key topics, or 2) review quarterly for refresher or continued development based on new needs, feedback or opportunity.

"The secret of getting ahead is getting started. The secret of getting started is breaking your complex overwhelming tasks into small manageable tasks, and then starting on the first one." - Mark Twain

Now, let's look at the Six Functions.

The Six Functions of Management focus on all "non-technical" areas of business management. Anything and everything you do as a manager will fall into one of these six buckets. A brief definition of each includes:

COMMUNICATING
CREATING UNDERSTANDING BETWEEN YOURSELF AND OTHERS

As a manager you constantly receive and provide information in a variety of communication formats, including oral, written and non-verbal. Building strong communication links across all levels of the organization is vital to your success.

PLANNING
DEFINING GOALS, SELECTING STRATEGIES AND CREATING ACTION PLANS

Almost all managerial activities are based on goals. Planning allows you to look ahead, map current and future goals and courses of action. Planning is a foundational activity which determines when, how and who is going to perform a specific activities, as well as action required in the future.

ORGANIZING
GROUPING TASKS AND RESOURCES TO ACHIEVE GOALS

Organizing is the function of management that piggybacks onto planning, where you identify tasks that need to be completed, select resources (human, mechanical, vendor and financial) needed to execute them and how to implement them effectively to reach goals successfully.

STAFFING

SELECTING, RETAINING, TRAINING AND COACHING

As a manager your ability to achieve goals without great people is limited. Therefore, you are responsible for development of staff, including proper and effective selection, appraisal and cultivation. If you aren't successful in attracting, hiring and retaining great staff, the other functions suffer.

CONTROLLING

MONITORING RESULTS, COMPARING TO PLAN AND TAKING CORRECTIVE ACTION

Controlling is about monitoring results, without micro-managing, to verify whether personal or team performance is meeting the standards set out in planning. Measuring progress against plan with a focus on taking corrective action helps ensure you hit business targets.

LEADING

DEVELOPING LEADER CHARACTERISTICS TO REACH TEAM AND ORGANIZATIONAL GOALS

Leading is the function in which managers develop self and team motivation to achieve goals. This includes development of personal leadership traits, functional teamwork, guiding, inspiring and instructing others towards the accomplishment of organizational goals.

"Seek to understand,
then to be understood"
- Stephen Covey

FUNCTION ONE

COMMUNICATING

All great communication begins with creating an understanding between yourself and others. Communication is the most utilized of all the Six Functions, and is the primary vehicle for conveying everything you want and need to do with and through others.

Successful managers have adaptable, consistent communication skills based on a variety of styles and delivery/receiving methods. Even proficient communicators can always find room for improvement.

Great communication depends on many factors—including style, frequency, pace, tone, timing etc.—to enable information sharing, decision making, influence, coordination, motivation, and identification of issues/opportunities. These also play a significant role in how others feel about you and their experience with you.

Everyone can develop the ability to shift their communication style to suit the needs of any given moment. Successfully modulating your style depends on your ability to:

1 Have awareness about your style and its impact on others

2 Observe and note the style of others around you

3 Adapt your communication in the moment

"Silence can never be misquoted"
- Unknown

Sounds easy, doesn't it? In reality, it can be very challenging to change your communication style. It can take time to modify a behavior so that it is consistent and sustained.

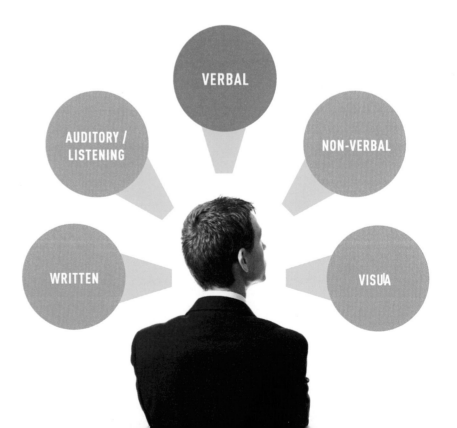

Why is communication so hard to change? We are creatures of habit. You are comfortable with your current style, and have been using it for a long time, likely with very little feedback on its effectiveness. Remember that communication success depends on how well your message is received. Adapting usually means you need to stop and think about what you want to say and how you will say it. Modifying your style will initially require a high level of self-awareness, partnered with conscious thought, consistent application and, ideally, getting feedback from others.

VERBAL – articulating thoughts to ensure your audience comprehends your message clearly and to manage conflict effectively

NON-VERBAL – awareness of your body language and its messaging to others

AUDITORY / LISTENING – demonstrating thoughtfulness, as well as increasing your ability to receive accurate information from others

WRITTEN – ability to articulate thoughts, plans and expectations in writing that is mapped appropriately to the audience(s) receiving the message

VISUAL – ability to read body language and non-verbal cues of others

HOW YOU
Interact with others

There are formal assessment tools that take the guesswork out of understanding your communication style and that of others, minimize the learning curve, and help get you the results you want sooner. One is DISC. This tool is easy to implement, use and understand. The on-line assessment takes 10-15 minutes, resulting in a 20 plus page personally tailored report. For now, let's get familiar with the DISC Model.

DISC AN OVERVIEW

DISC is an acronym for the four dimensions of human behavior: Dominance, Influencing, Steadiness and Compliance. We all have all four in our behavioral makeup, but how much of each we have can vary greatly.

In addition to helping you understand your preferred behavior and communication styles as well as others', this tool can help you in several key areas:

- Building stronger and more effective relationships

- Gaining credibility and influence

- Supporting conflict resolution and prevention

- Creating a positive, motivating environment

At a high level the DISC model explains:

DOMINANCE

HOW WE APPROACH PROBLEMS AND CHALLENGES

HIGH PERCENTAGE OF D: Extremely active and assertive when working to gain results, approaching challenge and opportunities with little to no fear.

LOWER PERCENTAGE OF D: Looks at challenges with a calculated, organized, well-thought out approach to gain desired results.

INFLUENCING

HOW WE INTERACT WITH OTHERS

HIGH PERCENTAGE OF I: Very high contact ability with people, outgoing, social, very verbally persuasive.

LOWER PERCENTAGE OF I: When approaching relationships with others, demonstrates a high level of caution, being very sincere and reserved. Very fact and information oriented.

STEADINESS

HOW WE HANDLE A STEADY PACE AND WORK ENVIRONMENT

HIGH PERCENTAGE OF S: Prefers a very structured, predictable environment with boundaries clearly defined.

LOWER PERCENTAGE OF S: Prefers an unstructured, undefined environment allowing for a great deal of freedom to operate.

COMPLIANCE

HOW WE RESPOND TO RULES AND REGULATIONS SET BY OTHERS

HIGH PERCENTAGE OF C: Follows rules set by others and is very aware of the affects of non-compliance with rules and procedures.

LOWER PERCENTAGE OF C: Prefers doing it 'my way', and establishing their own rules.

"All people exhibit all four behavioral factors in varying degrees of intensity"
- W.M. Marston

Should you decide to complete a formal assessment, your results will specifically outline your behavioral tendencies and percentages in these four areas. It is neither good nor bad to have high/low percentages in any specific dimension, but rather a way to look at your behavioral makeup.

Another advantage of DISC is its observability, meaning you can observe people and assess their predominant behavioral characteristics and appraise their style once you understand and can recall general characteristics for each profile. The grids on page (24-25) provide a more detailed perspective when assessing someone's style.

The illustration below looks at people from a high level and in two ways: across the top and vertically. Looking across the top at people with High C or D behavioral styles, we see they are more task/thinking focused and antagonistic. Across the bottom, people with High S and I profiles tend to be more favorable and feelings – relations-oriented.

Looking at the grid vertically, people with C and S as their primary behavioral style tend to be more introverted and passive whereas people with High D and I profiles are more extroverted or active. So a quick, high-level way to assess people's behavioral makeup is to ask "Is this person more task or people focused? Are they an introvert or an extrovert?"

Something to remember when utilizing DISC is that 96% of the population has a blending or combination of two to three styles; only 4% of profiles demonstrate a single style with one primary dimension. This grid provides a general guide, but keep in mind as you observe people that most will display tendencies from 2-3 of the descriptors.

	D DOMINANCE	I INFLUENCING	S STEADINESS	C COMPLIANCE
PSYCHOLOGICAL NEED	Direct, dominate others	Interact with others	Serve others	Comply with their own high standards
PREDOMINANT STRENGTH	High ego and task oriented	Optimistic and people-oriented	Team player, loyal, concrete results-oriented	Accuracy and highly intuitive
GOAL DRIVEN	Personal challenges	Social recognition	Traditional practices	Correct and proper way
FEAR	Being taken advantage of	Social rejection	Loss of security	Criticism of their work
OVER EXTENSION	Impatient	Disorganized	Possessive	Overly critical
COMMUNICATION	Fast paced and to the point	Motivational and inspiring	Patient, relaxed	Factual and to the point

After learning your own behavioral tendencies, the real work begins: applying the information to your interactions with others. People unfamiliar with the DISC model may not intuit your communication style or needs. For example, as a high D communicator, I prefer quick, to-the-point conversation and information. My employees may observe this about me over time but may not understand how to adapt to it fully. I find that if I tell them what I prefer, the learning curve shortens and communication improves more quickly. This tool has been useful throughout my career and has enhanced my ability to observe and adjust my own communication to other styles. When used in a balanced way, it is a very powerful and rewarding means to opening yourself to different communication styles and helping others adapt to your own, thereby increasing communication effectiveness very quickly!

The guidelines below are designed to help you interact and communicate with people according to their predominant DISC style:

COMMUNICATING WITH A HIGH D:

- Be direct, brief and to the point
- Focus on the task and stick to business
- Identify opportunities/challenges
- Use a logical approach
- Have a results-oriented approach
- Provide win/win situations
- Touch on high points and do not overuse data
- Do not physically touch. Keep a comfortable distance

COMMUNICATING WITH A HIGH I:

- Allow time for socialization
- Ask for feelings and opinions
- Expect quick decisions
- Lighten up and have fun
- Provide a friendly, non-threatening environment
- Use touch (forearm and back)
- Involve in brainstorming new ideas and approaches
- Provide opportunities for recognition and reward

COMMUNICATING WITH A HIGH S:

- Be patient
- Provide a logical approach to the facts
- Show how solutions will benefit them
- Involve them in planning
- Draw out their opinions
- Relax and allow time for discussion
- Clearly define all areas

COMMUNICATING WITH A HIGH C:

- Use data and facts
- Disagree with the facts, not the person
- Focus on quality
- Allow time for them to think
- Examine argument from all sides
- Keep on task and don't socialize
- Avoid 'new' solutions, stick to the proven ideas

MASTERING DISC

Mastering anything takes time, with a focus on application and repeated practice. Full mastery of this tool requires:

- Consistent use and application

- Observing and associating others styles

- Adapting your style to others

Since this is an 'observable' tool, you can associate traits with behavior to identify another's style. From there you adapt and are on your way to more effective communication.

If you do not know your behavioral style and are interested in finding out, follow the link below to inquire about ordering the DISC assessment.

 http://www.thesixfunctions.com/disc

HANDLING CONFLICT

Effectively handling conflict is a common management challenge; we all face this aspect of business life, but few of us enjoy having to deal with it. 85% of the managers I have polled in our programs have not received formal training on how to deal with and manage conflict. So where do managers learn this skill? Mostly through personal experience, trial and error, and observing others handling it.

Managed incorrectly, conflict can damage or break professional relationships. As relationship-building and people management is a key success factor for managers, Thomas-Kilmann's instrument, the TKI "Five Modes of Conflict" model, is an excellent assessment tool for better understanding and learning to manage conflict. This assessment is easy to take and provides a personal report on your preferred or most commonly used conflict modes along with tips and techniques to consider for making changes.

TWO BASIC ASPECTS OF ALL
CONFLICT HANDLING
MODES

To better handle conflict, understand your preferred modes, observe the mode others are in and adjust your mode based on the situation at hand.

THE FIVE MODES OF CONFLICT

At its essence, Kilmann defines conflict as: "Any situation where your desires or preferences differ from those of another."

According to Kilmann there are two basic dimensions that define the model: **(1)** assertiveness, the extent to which the person attempts to satisfy their own concerns, and **(2)** cooperativeness, the extent to which the person attempts to satisfy the other person's concerns. The Five Modes live within this two dimensional grid area. For example, Competing Mode is located at the top left grid, which indicates this mode is highly assertive with low cooperativeness. Collaboration is in the top right grid and indicates high assertiveness and cooperativeness levels. Compromising is mid-grid and has a balance of assertiveness and cooperativeness. Accommodating is bottom right grid and is low assertive but highly cooperative, and Avoiding is low on both

From "Conflict and Conflict Management," by Kenneth Thomas in Handbook of Industrial and Organizational Psychology edited by Marvin D. Dunnette, 1976, p. 900. Reprinted with permission of the editor.

dimensions. This is a high level look at the model. A more detailed review of the model is included in an on-line assessment report and includes; skill sets needed to effectively use each mode, overuse and under-use of each and the effects of both on you and others. The use of this model and assessment can help you; 1) understand your "go-to" modes and how to exercise using other modes for different conflict situations, 2) help you evaluate what mode another party is in so you can identify and adjust, and 3) allows you to better look at situations and select an appropriate mode(s) to enhance conflict outcomes. Take a moment to review the model and consider which are your Primary and Secondary modes used most often.

Outlined below are the tag line, primary goal and applications for each mode.

COMPETING MODE

"It's my way or the highway"

PRIMARY GOAL: To win. Grid Position: High assertiveness, Low cooperativeness. Applications for Competing mode include:

- **ASSERTING YOUR POSITION** – Standing up for your interests and ideas, making sure they are taken seriously
- **POSSIBILITY OF QUICK VICTORY** – Making a quick recommendation, pressing for a quick decision if you have enough power to prevail
- **SELF-DEFENSE** – Protecting your interests and views from attack
- **TESTING ASSUMPTIONS** – Debating to expose and test your own and others' assumptions

COLLABORATING MODE

"Two heads are better than one"

PRIMARY GOAL: Win-win. Grid Position: High assertiveness, High cooperativeness. Applications for Collaborating mode include:

- **HIGH-QUALITY DECISIONS** – Seeking innovative solutions that are better than each person's recommendation (Synergy)
- **LEARNING AND COMMUNICATION** – Exchanging information openly, aiding communication and discovery
- **RESOLUTION AND COMMITMENT** – Working toward meeting both people's concerns fully so that conflict is resolved and people are committed to the decision
- **STRENGTHENING RELATIONSHIPS** – Building respect and trust, resolving problems in a relationship

COMPROMISING MODE

"Let's make a deal"

PRIMARY GOAL: Find a middle ground. Grid Position: Mid assertiveness, mid cooperativeness. Applications for Compromising mode include:

- **PRAGMATISM** – Practicing the art of the possible, getting a deal that's good enough
- **SPEED AND EXPEDIENCY** – Making expedient settlements
- **FAIRNESS** – Providing equal gains and losses for both people
- **MAINTAINING RELATIONSHIPS** – Meeting halfway to reduce the strain on relationships

AVOIDING MODE

"I'll think about it tomorrow"

PRIMARY GOAL: To delay. Grid Position: Low assertiveness, Low cooperativeness. Applications for Avoiding mode include:

- **REDUCING STRESS** – Avoiding demanding or unpleasant people and topics
- **SAVING TIME** – Not wasting time and energy on low priority issues
- **STEERING CLEAR OF DANGER** – Not stirring up a hornets' nest or provoking trouble
- **SETTING UP MORE FAVORABLE CONDITIONS** – Gaining time to be better prepared, less distracted

ACCOMMODATING MODE

"It would be my pleasure"

PRIMARY GOAL: To yield. Grid Position: Low assertiveness, High cooperativeness. Applications for Accommodating mode include:

- **HELPING SOMEONE OUT** – Helping people, meeting their needs, supporting them
- **RESTORING HARMONY** – Smoothing feathers, calming troubled waters
- **BUILDING RELATIONSHIPS** – Building social capital by doing favors, helping, apologizing when necessary
- **CHOOSING A QUICK ENDING** – Cutting your losses so you can move on

After identifying your Primary and Secondary modes, think of a situation that involved conflict and identify the person and conflict mode you exhibited.

Now think about patterns of behavior based on specific people or situations. If you could change the mode you use in order to create a more positive outcome in future conflicts, what would it be? Fill in the blanks below!

SITUATION/PERSON	CURRENT/PAST MODE	OPPORTUNITY - FUTURE MODE

While a more extensive learning experience for this tool is delivered in half and full day programs, you can gain a basic understanding of your preferences along with an overview of each of your modes by obtaining a personal assessment.

http://www.thesixfunctions.com/tki

Conflict is a healthy aspect of human interaction. Too little conflict can create artificial harmony, while hurtful mean conflict can tear relationships apart. Managing conflict effectively balances these two extremes.

OTHER ASPECTS OF COMMUNICATION

Recognizing that you have opportunity to improve areas of your communication is important. Several example topics are presented, followed by a self-assessment section that will provide specific areas of focus.

DIFFICULT CONVERSATIONS

Do you experience fear or dread when you need or want to discuss something uncomfortable with a peer, direct report, or your manager?

Most people have a distaste discussing difficult topics. We tell ourselves: "If I bring this up "they might react like...", "Maybe if I wait until the end of the week they will bring this up...." The "what ifs" may stall those difficult, important conversations; the problem is, in the absence of direct communication and clear information, the human tendency is to fill in the blanks with assumptions. We are tentative about bringing up an uncomfortable topic, and trust others to "just know" how we feel. Unfortunately, there are not many people with mind reading on their resume!

One technique for conquering the anxiety about difficult conversations is to ask yourself "What is the worst that can happen if I bring up the topic?" Another technique is to begin by admitting your anxiety: "You know Sam; I have been hesitant to talk to you about this point because I wasn't sure how to start the conversation. If you are open to receiving feedback on this, I believe it would benefit us both." After getting affirmation to continue, you can follow up with specifics: "I would like to discuss the level of commitment we have on this project and to better understand your position before providing mine."

What do you do if the other person resists opening a dialogue? A follow-up might sound like: "I understand and appreciate you being truthful with me. This is an important topic and I want to ensure we both have an opportunity to get clarity and be on the same page moving forward. When would be a good time this week to dedicate an hour to this discussion?" This approach acknowledges and respects their position and also allows you to state yours and create a commitment to conversation. Sometimes people need to prepare or be in a better state of mind for these types of discussions.

Wrapping the message in a thoughtful, positive manner – staying on topic and removing emotion – will help solidify a win/win for everyone.

REQUESTING FEEDBACK

Asking for direct feedback is tough. Many people see asking for direct feedback as a weakness. However, one habit of a great manager is to consistently encourage feedback on their communication effectiveness. This step supports and models openness to personal development and creativity with your team; additionally, in the right context, it can increase motivation and inspiration. Remember the last time your manager or executive

"Truly great leaders spend as much time collecting and acting upon feedback as they do providing it." - Alexander Lucia

asked for your feedback on something? It showed that they respect you enough to listen, acknowledge and (when/if appropriate) act on your ideas. If you have experienced this, you know it is a great feeling.

What is stopping or discouraging you from asking for feedback? Often people that I coach or train experience two obstacles: 1) They are really anxious about what they will hear, and 2) they believe asking for feedback is a weakness. If the requested feedback is negative, our non-verbal, self-talk excuses flow: "Their perception is wrong"; "That person just doesn't know me or understand my position"; "He feels that he is smarter than I am and wants to show me up"; "We use to be peers and I was promoted; now she is jealous". Wouldn't it be great to perceive feedback as a gift, to adjust 'our' perceptions? Looking at each of these excuses provides an opportunity to change that perception and demonstrate active learning.

THEIR PERCEPTION IS WRONG – Perceptions are reality. People can be wrong, but their perception is their reality. If you ask for it, consider their point of view before negating it.

THAT PERSON DOESN'T KNOW ME OR UNDERSTAND MY POSITION – Maybe they don't. Conversation opens the door to understanding perspectives and without it, assumptions are made.

HE FEELS HE IS SMARTER THAN ME AND WANTS TO SHOW ME UP – Maybe they are smarter than you or demonstrate greater abilities in some areas. If that is the case, how can you leverage that for the benefit of the team or organization? Maybe your perception of their response is incorrect. Considering the core of their message may be of value.

WE USE TO BE PEERS AND I WAS PROMOTED; NOW SHE IS JEALOUS – Unfavorable feedback may stem from jealousy or hurt feelings over being passed up for promotion. However, acknowledging and addressing it creates discussion and the possibility of moving forward. Most times people just need to vent how they feel and can get past negative feelings.

ENCOURAGING FEEDBACK FROM OTHERS

Requesting or encouraging feedback can:

- Support open dialogue, as opposed to a one-sided conversation

- Allow for exploring others' points of view, opening up new possibilities

- Demonstrate to others that, as a leader, you do not need to appear all-knowing

- Help you become aware of 'blind spots' specific to your department or the organization

Working to obtain others' feedback allows you to take ownership and accountability for your communication planning and actions. It provides infrastructure for effective personal development planning. I am not recommending you encourage feedback on every management decision you make, but avoiding entirely it may cause you to become isolated or make others feel excluded from your decision-making process.

LISTENING

"No man ever listened himself out of a job."
— Calvin Coolidge

Listening is something we do all the time, consciously and subcons–ciously. Considering that the brain is basically an organic computer system, we are always in a state of thinking, talking, observing, reacting to things around us – all while listening. It is amazing that we can actually take in information clearly! Because we listen constantly, this aspect of communication sounds easy, but is one of the hardest to do really well. Some people are just naturally good listeners. Others struggle with it. There are various factors, including our different behavioral styles, how our brains are hard wired, that impact listening skills. The good news is that as human beings we have the ability to manage our senses and get focused on one set of stimuli or input response. Therefore we can set the stage for good listening by eliminating or reducing the distractions and stimuli that can get us off track during communication.

Eliminating distractions can include muting phones and computers, shutting computer screens off, and minimizing outside visual stimulus when engaging in important conversations.

In addition, it is important to understand that there is listening and there is active listening. Active listening is more than just hearing what people say; it includes acknowledging, paraphrasing, confirming and retaining what you have heard. For example: "I believe that point is key to Jim and his team. To be sure I am clear about your point, what I heard you say was……. Does that sound right?" If you can practice active listening skills, regardless of what's going on around you, then you will have made a big step towards and will soon see the value of focused, concentrated conversations. You will better understand what people are saying.

Enhancing your listening skills can make the difference in building solid relationships within and outside of your teams, increasing productivity and reducing mistakes and misunderstandings.

COMMUNICATING EXPECTATIONS

Nothing is worse than believing others know what you have in mind, only to find out that wasn't the case at all. Communicating expectations is important as it sets a standard for people and teams. Providing clearer expectations is another of the most common areas for improvement I see in 360 feedback reports for managers and leaders.

Consistent repetition of goals, performance standards and expectations increases retention rates. Stating expectations once or twice is not going to be enough; messages that stick with people are a result of repeated, consistent communication. Anything that disrupts active listening in others will diminish the likelihood your message will be heard.

Providing clear expectations consistently creates a baseline for measuring performance and results. It also provides clarity for a team, removes ambiguity and minimizes assumptions.

As a communicator, a consistent and regular message may begin to feel like a broken record. The reality is that people need consistent repetition for a message to sink in and stick.

A TRUE STORY

ADAPTING TO DIFFERENT COMMUNICATION STYLES

When I was operating my mail order business, I had an office manager who was very good on the phone, very talkative and friendly. While her style worked well for clients, it did less for me. She had a tendency toward long conversations and storytelling. I am a high Driver (in the DISC model) and prefer shorter, quick, "get to the point" conversation in the work environment. When Lisa had an issue with a shipment, she would begin the story with when the phone rang and tell me every detail of what this client ordered and why. After a few months of listening to drawn out explanations of business events and issues, I finally stopped her right in the middle of a story with a "time out" hand signal. She asked, "What's wrong?" and I replied "Lisa, I don't need the whole story for every issue we have in the business. All I need to know is what the problem is." She said that her husband often had the same complaint. I suggested that she keep her narrative to a brief description of the problem; I would ask for more detail if necessary. She agreed moving forward that she would try to honor more direct communication. Her e-mail style also tended to be long and drawn out, I requested that these be brief as well, short and to the point with no more than 3-5 bullet points.

Weeks passed and she made a genuine effort to adapt to my preferred communication style. If she came in to describe a problem and started in storytelling mode, all I had to do was say, "Lisa" in a higher pitched tone, and she immediately knew what I wanted. She would adjust and give me the bottom line. Now here's the flip side of the story...

As I began to look at my communication with Lisa, I saw that she had adapted her communication style in a way that worked for me. But what about what she needed and wanted from me? I realized that when she came in every day, I would give her a brief hello and get on to business, requesting the daily reports. I willingly began to adapt my communication to her preferences. She appreciated the gesture, and would respect my needs and joke, "I know you just want your reports but thank you for asking."

MORAL OF THE STORY: Communicate what you want from people and ask what they need from you. We all have communication preferences and most times we are hoping others will be receptive enough to identify and adjust to meet those needs.

COMMUNICATING SKILLS ASSESSMENT

The self-assessment that follows comes from Kerr Hill's Managers Performance Program 360 feedback survey. It is a starting point to benchmark key focus areas for enhancing your communication style. In a traditional 360 survey, these questions go out to people around you (your manager, peers, directs reports) to aggregate information on how your sense of your communications skills compares to their perception of you.

Take a moment to think about each question and rate yourself on the scale provided. While reflecting on these areas, try not to over-analyze your answer. The goal here is to look at and recognize high scores as strengths and determine areas of improvement in your communication performance. Guidelines for totaling and assessing your score are on the previous page.

TOTAL AND INDIVIDUAL SCORE GUIDELINES

You can evaluate your communication effectiveness in the following assessment two ways; 1) by comparing your overall average score against the scale below and 2) by looking at specific scores in each category. The specific score topics will then become personal goal focal points for action planning in the last part of this section. Remember: don't take on too much, learn to modulate change – it's better to master one area of change than to try and change a variety of things with less success.

Total Average Score Guidelines (Total Average score is complied by adding up all the individual scores and dividing by the number of questions.)

1-2 **Low Skill Level** - Your overall communication skills need improvement. Select one topic to action plan first.

3-4 **Adequate to Proficient** - Communication skills are good and some may still have opportunity for further development.

5 **Excellent - Natural Strength** - Overall you are an excellent communicator.

Evaluate yourself in the areas below by assigning a 1 to 5 score on the following questions:

1 I provide clear, concise verbal directions and explanations:

| 1 POOR ☐ | 2 FAIR ☐ | 3 AVERAGE ☐ | 4 GOOD ☐ | 5 EXCELLENT ☐ |

2 I communicate in writing clearly and concisely:

| 1 POOR ☐ | 2 FAIR ☐ | 3 AVERAGE ☐ | 4 GOOD ☐ | 5 EXCELLENT ☐ |

3 I provide clear, defining expectations:

| 1 POOR ☐ | 2 FAIR ☐ | 3 AVERAGE ☐ | 4 GOOD ☐ | 5 EXCELLENT ☐ |

4 I demonstrate attentive listening:

| 1 POOR ☐ | 2 FAIR ☐ | 3 AVERAGE ☐ | 4 GOOD ☐ | 5 EXCELLENT ☐ |

5 I encourage feedback from others (peers, management, clients, etc):

| 1 POOR ☐ | 2 FAIR ☐ | 3 AVERAGE ☐ | 4 GOOD ☐ | 5 EXCELLENT ☐ |

6 I keep others informed:

| 1 POOR ☐ | 2 FAIR ☐ | 3 AVERAGE ☐ | 4 GOOD ☐ | 5 EXCELLENT ☐ |

7 I handle conflict effectively and in timely fashion:

| 1 POOR ☐ | 2 FAIR ☐ | 3 AVERAGE ☐ | 4 GOOD ☐ | 5 EXCELLENT ☐ |

8 I am sensitive to non-verbal cues (body language, facial expressions):

| 1 POOR ☐ | 2 FAIR ☐ | 3 AVERAGE ☐ | 4 GOOD ☐ | 5 EXCELLENT ☐ |

9 I demonstrate respect for others' points of view:

| 1 POOR ☐ | 2 FAIR ☐ | 3 AVERAGE ☐ | 4 GOOD ☐ | 5 EXCELLENT ☐ |

TOTAL AVERAGE SCORE: ☐

Total all scores and divide by 9

Choose one to three topics that have low scores (3 or less) to consider creating an action plan on for continued development. Even if you had scores in the 4 range, consider those as opportunities for growth. If you had scores in the 5's, be aware that with any area of strength, if overused, it can be perceived by others as a weakness. Specific score topics I will focus on:

1

2

3

In addition to this self scoring tool, there are other ways in which to assess how you are communicating, some of which we have reviewed in this section:

- Asking directly for feedback from others

- Using a workplace assessment or survey tool (360 Feedback or other Human Resources Survey tools)

- Taking a personal behavior assessment profile – DISC, TKI or others

- Attending facilitated communication courses that include feed–back reviews

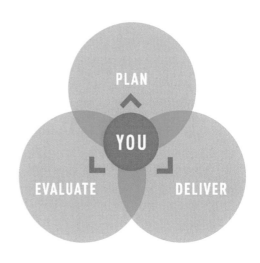

MAKING COMMUNICATION CHANGES

Now that you have rated yourself and have a perspective on both strengths and areas for improvement, it's time to take things to the next level through action planning.

Easy and comfortable habits are the hardest things for people to change. Changing comfort zone behavior isn't easy, but neither is it impossible. I have seen many professionals make significant behavioral changes with very positive benefits to themselves and their teams.

Two things happen when you prepare to change any aspect of your management style:

1   You must stop or slow down and think about what you are doing differently. Habits come easy and die hard. Initially, a new pattern will take a little more focused thought, which is okay.

2   It will feel uncomfortable or unnatural to do something different. Repetition of a new habit will soon make it feel natural. Stephen Covey says it takes 21 days of consistent practice to change a habit. So be patient with yourself and don't give up. You may have to tweak an aspect of what you do to make it just right, but so be it.

THE IGOA_{SM} ACTION PLANNING PROCESS

Most people take a goal and move right into action planning. The IGOA_{SM} process changes this tendency and has you look at a core issue more closely and focuses on obstacles when creating action plans for goal attainment.

IGOA_{SM} is an acronym for a four-part action planning process. The I stands for Issue and what is at the core of generating a goal. The G stands for Goal or the end result you are trying to achieve regarding the issue at hand. The O stands for Obstacles, which are the things that will or may get in your way of achieving the goal. The A stands for Action Plans, the specific actions you are going to take to overcome obstacles and achieve your goal.

The IGOA_{SM} action planning process was designed as time limited action planning that can be done on your own, with another person, or in a team/group environment. This process was created at Kerr Hill and has been successfully used for over 22 years, assisting managers, leaders and teams to identify and attain goals in a systematic manner. You will find that it is simple, can be quickly assimilated and easily shared and adopted by others.

To avoid over-thinking, you should not spend more than 15 minutes on creating an IGOA_{SM}. Below is the suggested timing:

- 1 minute to identify the ISSUE

- 1 minute to state the GOAL

- 5 minutes to identify OBSTACLES to the goal

- 8 minutes to create ACTION ITEMS – activities to overcome obstacles

To implement on your own, use the steps below. If you are involving others in the IGOA_{SM} process, you must provide them an overview of what you are doing and why.

Using the IGOAsm worksheet and a timer (remember the 15 minute rule), find a quiet location to craft your plan. To get started, use a blank piece of paper to note all pertinent information that may feed into the process.

ON THE IGOAsm FORM PROVIDED:

- Write a clear, concise Issue statement. Example: **"I don't encourage enough feedback."**

- Write a personal development Goal addressing your issue: **"I will be perceived as a manager who encourages more feedback by May 30, 2014."**

- List Obstacles you may experience in reaching the goal, and then **rank the top three with a 1, 2 and 3**.

- **Brainstorm and create Action Items you will implement** to overcome each obstacle and achieve the goal. Be sure to fill out who will help you with action items and when you will begin each action item. Remember to check your time.

- **Keep in mind** that the more you do it, the easier it becomes, and the faster you can complete it. You will get to a point where you will be doing this in your head and won't need the worksheet as often, if at all.

SAMPLE IGOA_{SM} FORM FILLED OUT:

ISSUE:	I don't encourage enough feedback.

GOAL:	I will be perceived as a manager who encourages more feedback by May 30, 2014.

OBSTACLES: to attain my goal

I'm impatient (1)	People don't give me feedback when I ask
Lack of time	I may be intimidating
Poor listening skills (2)	
Fear of getting negative feedback (3)	

ACTION PLAN: focused in overcoming my top 3 obstacles, which will get me to my goal

ACTION ITEM	WHO	WHEN
Slow down and stay in the moment when asking for feedback.	Me	5/1/14
Engage in active listening. Have a notepad and pen when asking for feedback and take notes. Turn off all other distractions.	Me	5/1/14
Be open to feedback as a positive leader trait and bury the negative fear associated with it. Learn from it versus running from it.	Me	5/5/14
Give people permission to provide feedback without recourse. Explain that without it, things cannot change for the better.	Me	5/7/14
Be aware of my body language and responses so that people are not intimidated by me.	Me	5/1/14

From the three areas of improvement you selected at the top of page 42, or from your self assessment scoring, select one specific topic you would like to improve on and use the following IGOAsm Worksheet for developing a Communicating goal and improvement action plan.

ISSUE:

GOAL:

OBSTACLES: to attain my goal

_____   _____

_____   _____

_____   _____

ACTION PLAN: focused in overcoming my top 3 obstacles, which will get me to my goal

ACTION ITEM	WHO	WHEN

FUNCTION 1
COMMUNICATING REVIEW

What do great communicators do consistently? They listen, confirm and clarify what they heard, state their position and gain commitment with clear expectations.

We have covered the function of Communicating from a variety of angles. Communication is the primary vehicle by which you send and receive information. There are many variables, considerations and influencing factors in being an effective communicator.

Successful managers understand, care about and practice their skills in this management function.

If you have ever worked with someone who is a well-rounded, effective communicator, you know firsthand how much easier life can be for you.

To summarize this section we have explored the following:

- Personal behavior styles and communication preferences with DISC

- The Thomas-Kilmann Instrument (TKI) for managing conflict

- Communication aspects including: difficult conversations, encouraging feedback, listening skills and communication expectations

- A self-assessment process designed to help you acknowledge strengths and areas for improvement

- A self-guided action planning process (IGOA$_{SM}$) as a tool to implement change

"To effectively communicate, we must realize that we are all different in the way we perceive the world and use this understanding as a guide to our communication with others."

- Tony Robbins

"A goal without a plan is just a wish."
— Antoine de Saint-Exupéry

CHAPTER HIGHLIGHTS

>>   PLANNING DEFINED

>>   SMART GOALS

>>   THE PARETO PRINCIPLE

>>   CREATING A POWER HOUR

"Strategy lives in the space between where you are at and where you want to be."

FUNCTION TWO

PLANNING

DEFINING GOALS, SELECTING STRATEGIES AND CREATING ACTION PLANS

The function of planning creates the baseline or blueprint for what you want to accomplish in your role. This includes what goals, strategies and related action plans you need to execute. A well-designed plan can help you and your organization achieve its mission. Effective planning will sharpen your focus, prioritize strategies and implement the changes you want to realize.

There are basically two types of planning: short term and long term. Short term planning is typically focused at 12 months or less and long term on 12 months or more.

Many managers tend focus on shorter-term plans, meaning weekly, monthly or quarterly. This is very common, as it is essentially what they have been hired to do. C suite executives often stay focused on longer term, broader picture planning, to keep the company on track with emerging market and competitor trends. This longer-term perspective provides a lens for future goals. From a day-to-day, month-to-month perspective, your planning should align with and support the organizational strategic goals.

ENVISION YOUR ORGANIZATION'S GOALS

Creating a vision and setting crisp SMART business goals helps clarify the objectives of the organization and supports the mission. This should take shape as a detailed, written document, connecting the planning activity with your mission statement and services. This becomes your compass when moving forward with all planning activity.

Aspects of planning to consider:

- **PRIORITIZING** – ranking initiatives properly, understanding what has the greatest impact and value to you and your team, allocating resources needed to support those initiatives

- **STRATEGIZING** – ability to explore different methods of reaching goals and selecting the best. Being able to brainstorm and think outside the box with new approaches to goal attainment

- **OBSTACLES** – inhibitors to goal attainment. Look for roadblocks before they occur, and determine if they can be turned into supporting opportunities, proactive vs. reactive

- **PROBLEM SOLVING** – skill needed for creating solutions to overcoming obstacles. Work through problems; don't ignore them. Involve others if you can't get creative on your own

- **ACTION PLANNING** – create and implement action plans specific to the strategies and opportunities identified

Most people confuse tactics for strategy. Tactics are specific action items that live within a strategy. Strategy is the overall game plan or way you want to approach attaining a goal.

SETTING SMART GOALS

The word Goal can be defined as: An end result to be achieved.

Successful planning starts with having clear, realistic goals. When creating a goal statement, it should be focused on 'end results' rather than language on the process of attainment, who is involved or any action steps. A good, concise sample goal statement will be reviewed in the following SMART goals definitions.

Creating SMART business goals can positively impact you, your team and projects. So, what is meant by SMART? It is an acronym for the 5 elements that make up great focused goals.

SPECIFIC – Make sure that the goal is specific and not vague. It must be obvious when you read it. The test for this is that a casual reader should finish reading it with a fairly complete understanding of what you are trying to accomplish. Overly complex phrasing such as "we want to increase productivity to help increase the output of orders every day so that we satisfy customer needs" should be avoided. Forgo run-on sentences in favor of a specific business goal statement.

If your goal is to increase customer satisfaction, then a specific goal statement should sound like "I will Increase customer satisfaction by 10% by 4/30/2014".

MEASURABLE – It sounds simple (and many business goals are easily measured), but certain things such as increasing productivity can be harder to measure. My belief is that everything can be measured in one way or another. There are easy metrics for things such as increasing sales by 12% within the next 30 days. However, something like increasing productivity can be more challenging to gauge; such measurement is made easier with prior data on output, quality or time to completion. Without prior data you must create a new baseline through measurement.

A good productivity goal should sound like; "I will increase team productivity by 15% by 9/30/2014". Measuring results in this case will rely on measuring output between now and the end of the goal period. Increasing team productivity means that a team can do more, in less time, with the same number of resources or resource constraints.

ACHIEVABLE – Can the goal be achieved? If the immediate answer is "Yes, no problem, hands down," that may be a sign that the goal isn't challenging enough. However if there is an

immediate, overwhelming "NO!" the goal may be too lofty and unattainable. Aim to balance between the two extremes, calling those just slightly out of reach stretch goals. Stretch goals are achievable, but are not too easy or comfortable to attain.

Take time to look at past goals. Have you been easily meeting them all, just missing or completely missing them?

RELEVANT – Is the goal relevant to your job, the team's charter, management objectives or organizational goals? If you are not sure, then before you do anything else, get clarity! If you are clear on the goal, but do not see how it fits into the bigger picture, it is a great opportunity to meet with your manager or management team to gain clarity.

EXAMPLE: Reducing office supply costs is a good business goal assuming the CEO has put out a company-wide memo stating he/she wants everyone to reduce office supply expenses by 25%. It may not be a relevant goal if the CEO has just asked everyone to increase productivity in order to stay competitive in the market.

Get SMART with your goals!

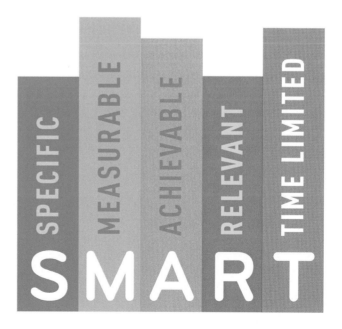

SPECIFIC MEASURABLE ACHIEVABLE RELEVANT TIME LIMITED

SMART

TIME LIMITED - In my trainings, I consistently hear business goals stated without time and date stamps. A goal statement without a time-line is a moving target with no likely end. Wanting to increase quality, productivity or other business metrics by a certain percent sounds great, but if you don't have a time marker for the goal, is it really going to be achieved and measurable? Saying "due by the end of next week" is a good example of a poor time limited statement.

If you date and time-bound it, then you know exactly what you need to do and by when!

SHORT TERM BUSINESS GOALS

Now that we have reviewed SMART goals, let's put it into practice.

Writing and communicating business goals is important not only for your own focus, but provides transparency and clarity for direct reports, peers and other organizational teams. We have all read business goals written in long paragraphs, touching on multiple topics and going into detail as to why the goal exists.

Less is more when it comes to articulating short-term goals. Below is an example of a short term, SMART goal. It crisp and to the point!

"I will reduce error rates in data entry in the ABC department by 25% over last month by 3/31/2014." Breaking it down into the SMART format:

- SPECIFIC to reduce date entry errors in ABC department
- MEASURABLE 25% reduction rate
- ACHIEVABLE realistic target amount was set
- RELEVANT supports department and organizational goals
- TIME LIMITED has a specific date stamp on it

I prefer to have short term business goals use 30 days as the time-frame for completion. There are multiple reasons for this, the primary being that 30 days is a realistic time frame to set and measure goals. Another advantage to 30 day goals is you can break them down into quarters or bite size components that become easier to achieve and measure. Aside from making it easy to map to the fiscal calendar year, short-term goals also create focus, urgency and a segue to the next area of business improvement.

LONG TERM GOALS: TAKING STRATEGIC THINKING TIME

When I ask course participants how many of them actually take 'Strategic Thinking Time' – meaning time to pause, reflect and consider alternatives without engaging in regular work – I am amazed at how few do this. We often spend 99% of our time on day-to-day management of business affairs. How often should you consider pulling yourself out of out of that space and invest it in looking ahead a bit? What is down the road in the long term, 12 months or longer? What can you picture or perceive as future outcomes? If you had a magic wand and could create any outcome you wanted, what would that look like? When you take time to strategize you give yourself a chance to see what possibilities exist.

Sharing vision can be hard, as others can't always see what you have in your mind's eye. But if you have a clear vision that resonates inside you, it can be explained and people will get it.

GAINING CLARITY

THE PARETO PRINCIPLE & POWER HOUR

The Pareto Principle was derived from a mathematician who lived in Italy in the late 1800's. His name was Alfredo Pareto. The Italian government hired him to conduct wealth distribution surveys, meaning they wanted to know who and how wealth was distributed across the country. Pareto went out and conducted door to door census intakes and when he concluded, he found that 20% of the population held 80% of the wealth. The government then started looking at businesses. They also found 80% of a businesses revenue came from just 20% of its customer base. Thus the "Pareto Principle" or the 80/20 rule was coined. The Power Hour is a derivative of the Pareto Principle designed to have you create dedicated time for focusing on high priority items, or your "critical few" tasks. Following this, 80% of your results can be gained through focusing on the 20% most critical few tasks. Are you making time every day to stay focused on the most critical 20% your job? If not, then implementing a Power Hour may help you achieve it.

CREATING A PARETO PRINCIPLE POWER HOUR

Applying the Pareto Principle to your day entails about a 2-hour commitment, two hours to focus on the critical few things that make the biggest impact on your business or team results. This can include taking time for coaching team members, meeting with peers to build relationships, managing up, and creating new strategies; if you contribute to technical work, that includes finding isolated focus time for that as well. We arrive at creating a power hour each day by breaking down a 50-hour work week.

This would look like:

50 HOURS X 20% = 10 HOURS A WEEK

10 HOURS / 5 DAYS = 2 HOURS A DAY

If you break the two hours into an AM Power Hour and a PM Power Hour you can get your "20%" time in each day.

The most important aspect of incorporating this technique is dedicating time to regularly complete it. If 2 hours daily seems impossible, break it down into smaller segments of perhaps 20-30 minutes for a Power 20 or 30.

Planning takes time, thinking time. Many people do not feel productive if they are not doing a task. Taking thinking time to plan effectively is doing something very important.

SELF COMMITMENT
POWER HOUR

A.M. POWER HOUR	TIME:	PLACE:
A.M. POWER 20/30	TIME:	PLACE:

P.M. POWER HOUR	TIME:	PLACE:
P.M. POWER 20/30	TIME:	PLACE:

Create your commitment to a Power Hour or Power 20-30 below.

TIP: Ask yourself, When is my best time during the day to get my best work done? "How do I get the time and keep it?" Consider measures such as carving out time and hanging a sign on your door stating you are in a Power Hour or try and find a quiet office or meeting space where you won't be interrupted.

When planning your Power Hour, think about the critical few things you want to focus on for that day, tomorrow and long term to improve your level of success. These could include, but are not limited to:

- Strategy – Organizational or Departmental
- Coaching/Development of Direct Reports
- Building Organizational Relationships
- Brainstorming
- Technical Work
- Managing Up/Communication

A TRUE STORY:

MISSING MARKET OPPORTUNITIES

When I was designing, manufacturing and selling mobile office products (car desks, filing systems for vehicles) I had to juggle all the time – short term, long term thinking for product development, marketing, sales and inventory. I had 30 day plans and 6-18 month targets.

A new product could take 3-4 months to refine from inception to prototype to production. Aside from our own products, we were constantly on the lookout for other products on the market that were ready for resale. Our annual catalog would get updated every fall, so I had windows of time to target. I had all these variables and time-lines to deal with on an ongoing basis. With managing the manufacturing our line of products, I also had to manage our contracted manufacturing vendors and ensure they received all the raw materials for manufacturing. From there we had the products being branded with our logo and then finally we would have inventory. If I slipped or neglected to cover one aspect, the company might lose market share or an opportunity to present a new product to the market. I did not learn to plan in college; no one really sat me down and showed me how to do it. I learned by seat of the pants, by trial and error. There were several times where I delayed a product launch only to see a competitor's product out on the market ahead of ours. That hurt and I beat myself up for having lost sight of an important business responsibility. I swore something like this would never happen again, and it didn't. Through all of this I realized I liked the challenge and variety of the job, and I was fortunate enough to have natural planning skills to support the needs of the business. However, all it takes is to get bitten just once by the "lack of planning bug" and you will realize the impact it can have on you, your team and your business.

MORAL OF THE STORY: Spend time planning and ensure all your short- and long-term goals are covered. They are the blueprint for what you want to accomplish. Poor blueprints, poor execution, poor results.

PLANNING SKILLS REVIEW AND ASSESSMENT

The function of Planning is the most important baseline component of management. Setting goals, selecting strategies and subsequent action plans form a road map for moving you, your team and the business forward. Below are items to use as reminders for effective planning as well as an assessment to help you focus on areas of opportunity and improvement.

- Plan using SMART and create crisp goal statements

- Identify whether the planning is for short- or long-term goals

- Apply the Pareto Principle to separate out the Critical from Trivial

- Block out your Power Hour time to focus on the most important aspects of your job

1 I foresee problems and opportunities:

1 POOR	2 FAIR	3 AVERAGE	4 GOOD	5 EXCELLENT

2 I analyze situations well:

1 POOR	2 FAIR	3 AVERAGE	4 GOOD	5 EXCELLENT

3 I develop direction, including vision, mission and strategies:

1 POOR	2 FAIR	3 AVERAGE	4 GOOD	5 EXCELLENT

4 I ensure that work is clearly identified and scheduled:

1 POOR	2 FAIR	3 AVERAGE	4 GOOD	5 EXCELLENT

5 I lead in planning performance standards:

1 POOR	2 FAIR	3 AVERAGE	4 GOOD	5 EXCELLENT

6 I set clear goals and objectives:

1 POOR	2 FAIR	3 AVERAGE	4 GOOD	5 EXCELLENT

7 I develop practical action plans:

1 POOR	2 FAIR	3 AVERAGE	4 GOOD	5 EXCELLENT

8 I ensure priorities are set:

1 POOR	2 FAIR	3 AVERAGE	4 GOOD	5 EXCELLENT

TOTAL AVERAGE SCORE:

Total all scores and divide by 8

Now that you have your individual scores, select a specific topic area that is low and use the following IGOAsm Worksheet for creating a Planning development goal and action plan.

ISSUE:

GOAL:

OBSTACLES: to attain my goal

_____   _____

_____   _____

_____   _____

ACTION PLAN: focused in overcoming my top 3 obstacles, which will get me to my goal

ACTION ITEM	WHO	WHEN

"By failing to prepare, you are preparing to fail."

- Benjamin Franklin

FUNCTION THREE

ORGANIZING

We can't manage time, we can only learn to manage ourselves better to utilize time more effectively.

GROUPING TASKS AND RESOURCES TO ACHIEVE GOALS

Organizing is the function of management that follows and piggybacks onto planning, where you identify different tasks and resources needed to carry out the plan. Resources can include human, technical, machines, vendors and financial.

Most often when you hear the term "organizing" you immediately think about how clean your desk is, whether files are in their proper place, and if the office is in generally good, clean order. While these are important aspects of being organized, they are not the only way we look at this function. It really refers to assessing all tasks and projects you or your team need to accomplish, and to considering resources, availability, capacity, and abilities to reach the goal in the most efficient and effective manner.

To begin, you need to have a clear idea of all tasks that are required to achieve goals and to support business operations. Without clarity on your group tasks – who will be assigned, what resources will be requested and allotted – efficiency and effectiveness can be compromised. It is important to include your tasks in this mix.

Once you identify the tasks you will keep and which you will delegate, make assignments to the appropriate team members, vendors, and/or work groups.

GROUPING TASKS

ASSIGNING TASKS

ESTIMATING TIME

TEAM FEEDBACK

GET CLARITY

On average, people who can delegate effectively create anywhere from 25-40% more time in their schedule for their personal critical few tasks.

ASPECTS OF ORGANIZING TO CONSIDER:

- Group similar tasks together

- Identify strengths of individuals when assigning tasks

- Estimate time needed for tasks, including current time and future goals

- Allow for team member input related to the evaluation process, taking or sharing tasks

- Verbally, and in writing, confirm assigned tasks and resources to ensure clarity

Clearly identify roles and responsibilities for you, your team as a whole and your team members as individuals. Then structure the work:

- Identify primary functions of work

- Identify groups that like to work, and work well, together

- Organize around work, not people or titles

- Establish one supervising manager or team lead

- Reorganize work when appropriate

- When in doubt, don't reorganize

- When you do it, do it right

Remember to delegate with control:

- Look for work you are doing that can be performed by others

- Delegate in terms of results expected

- Determine task authority, limits within which to make decisions

- Create accountability, commitment to results

- Keep control – don't abdicate

- Seek buy-in (let others be involved in the 'How')

- Establish status updates

- Monitor regularly

- Expect people to take corrective action

- Reward results

- Trust yourself and others

- Learn from mistakes

ASSESSING AND DELEGATING TASKS

In the left "Tasks I Do" column, list all tasks that you currently perform at work. From this column, review and move the tasks which you can REALISTICALLY delegate and list those in the middle column ("Tasks I can Delegate"). These can be partial or full aspects of a task. Finally, whatever is left over from column one that was not delegated, should be listed in the far right column considered to be your "Critical Few". These are your core, most important tasks. (Note: your list may be much longer than the space provided here, so use a blank piece of paper if need be)

TASKS I DO	TASKS I CAN DELEGATE	MY CRITICAL FEW

 Until you value yourself, you won't value your time.
Until you value your time, you will not do anything with it.
- M. Scott Peck

CONSIDERATIONS FOR ESTIMATING TASK TIME

When thinking about how much time any task will take, it is a good rule of thumb to remember the 3 P's: Purpose, People and Process.

PURPOSE – Consider the impact on the organization, your department or group goals.

- What is the task purpose?
- Why is it important? How is it important to the organization or department?
- What would happen if it is not completed in a timely manner?

PEOPLE – Consider the 'who' to be involved: your team, customers, vendors, employees, personality types, values and beliefs.

- Who will affect or could be affected by the tasks?
- How would they be affected if it is not completed in a timely manner?

PROCESS – Consider all the information about how the company runs, efficiency of production, effectiveness of machinery, work environment and productivity.

- What is the current process?
- What would happen if it is not completed in a timely manner?

ESTIMATING TIME FOR CRITICAL FEW TASKS-EXERCISE PART 2

Write the Critical Few tasks from the Assessing and Delegating Tasks exercise from page 70 in the far left column below. In column two, (Time per week) estimate how much time per week you cumulatively spend on each task. In the "Ideal Per Week" column, list what you believe would be an ideal amount of time for each task, considering purpose, people and processes that may affect the estimated time. Finally, calculate the "% of Time" each task takes by dividing the Ideal Time by your hours worked per week. Example: Critical Few Task #1, Meetings: Time per week: 25 hours, Ideal per week: 15 hrs. % of Time is calculated; 15 hours / 50hrs worked = 30% of your time.

MY CRITICAL FEW TASKS	TIME PER WEEK	IDEAL PER WEEK	% MY OF TIME

Do you feel that you are investing the right amount of time in the proper areas?

How can you shift from current to ideal time for each task?

How can you manage time wasters that impact your critical few?

TIPS TO ORGANIZE YOURSELF

Prepare for tomorrow, today. Spend your last fifteen minutes at work cleaning up and getting organized for the next day. Make your 'To Do' list or checklist of tasks. Make sure to set priorities, gathering information and a list of resources.

Efficiency is getting a lot of things done. Effectiveness is getting all the right things done, correctly, the first time.

It has been documented that people who write a "to-do list" are 10 – 15% more productive than those who don't. Why? Those who organize:

- Know what they need to get done

- Can prioritize necessary tasks

- Contact those needed to help execute a plan in advance and secure their availability

- Allocate the appropriate amount of time to each task.

Prioritize tasks by focusing on assignments that must be done. Assign each task on your list a number from 1 to 5.

1 Must be done

2 Should be done

3 Would be nice to get done

4 Could be done another day

5 Doesn't really matter

During the day, focus on doing more ones and twos, and fewer fours and fives. By the end of the day, you may be surprised at your productivity, and how little time you wasted chasing around after things that can wait or don't really matter.

Be flexible to allow for changing priorities, problems and other unanticipated events.

A TRUE STORY

ASSESSING MY OFFICE MANAGER FOR EFFICIENCY

I once had an office manager who handled payroll, insurance, balancing the books, checking mail and handling other business-related projects I would give her. The job was part time and I had identified it should take 16-18 hours a week to complete all tasks. I had done many, if not all, of these tasks myself at one point, so I felt I had a realistic sense of the time needed. Yet she was taking 24 hours a week or more to complete her work. I could not figure out why, so we sat down for a discussion and listed her responsibilities.

I had her track time on each task for two weeks; we then sat down to review. I quickly spotted a lot of inefficiency: two hours for sorting through mail, three hours on email, etc. These seemed excessive for our level of volume. I perceived several possible reasons: A) she was doing her best but was unsuited for the tasks, therefore taking longer to complete them than me, B) she was taking her time to get hours in, C) she was socializing in the office, or D) all of the above.

After reviewing the results, we decided she should take a vacation for us both to think about whether this was the right job for her. Two weeks passed and we sat down in a private 1-on-1 session to see where we had landed. Before I got fully seated she said "You are going to fire me aren't you?" I got as far as the word "Well..." when she continued, "You can't, because I am quitting!" I agreed the best solution for us both was to part ways and it was done amicably.

MORAL OF THE STORY: Inspect what you expect and have very clear roles and responsibilities for yourself and your staff. Review from time to time as things change; recognize that people will create their own perceptions of what they should be doing and how long it should take them.

ORGANIZING SKILLS ASSESSMENT

The following assessment is one of many ways to evaluate your organizing skills. Other things to consider:

- Getting/asking for feedback from direct reports – are they all clear on their roles and tasks?

- When tasks are aligned property, is the amount of time they take reasonable? If not, consider conducting a task time survey.

- Are you holding onto and performing tasks others should be performing? If so why? How is this impacting your time management?

- Are you providing coaching and empowering others when delegating new tasks to them?

1 I structure work properly:

1 POOR	2 FAIR	3 AVERAGE	4 GOOD	5 EXCELLENT
☐	☐	☐	☐	☐

2 I obtain and utilize resources effectively:

1 POOR	2 FAIR	3 AVERAGE	4 GOOD	5 EXCELLENT
☐	☐	☐	☐	☐

3 I structure working relationships:

1 POOR	2 FAIR	3 AVERAGE	4 GOOD	5 EXCELLENT
☐	☐	☐	☐	☐

4 I establish clear roles and authority:

1 POOR	2 FAIR	3 AVERAGE	4 GOOD	5 EXCELLENT
☐	☐	☐	☐	☐

5 I integrate related activities:

1 POOR	2 FAIR	3 AVERAGE	4 GOOD	5 EXCELLENT
☐	☐	☐	☐	☐

6 I am able to sort the vital from the less important:

1 POOR	2 FAIR	3 AVERAGE	4 GOOD	5 EXCELLENT
☐	☐	☐	☐	☐

7 I delegate work:

1 POOR	2 FAIR	3 AVERAGE	4 GOOD	5 EXCELLENT
☐	☐	☐	☐	☐

8 I manage time effectively:

1 POOR	2 FAIR	3 AVERAGE	4 GOOD	5 EXCELLENT
☐	☐	☐	☐	☐

TOTAL AVERAGE SCORE:
Total all scores and divide by 8

Now that you have your individual scores, select a specific topic area that is low and use the IGOA℠ Worksheet for creating an Organizing focused goal and action plan.

ISSUE:

GOAL:

OBSTACLES: to attain my goal

ACTION PLAN: focused in overcoming my top 3 obstacles, which will get me to my goal

ACTION ITEM	WHO	WHEN

*"Being well organized allows you to
be both efficient and effective."*

- Eleanor Roosevelt

CHAPTER HIGHLIGHTS

>>   RECRUITING

>>   INTERVIEWING TIPS

>>   BEHAVIORAL INTERVIEWING QUESTIONS

>>   COACHING

FUNCTION FOUR

STAFFING

CFO asks CEO: "What happens if we invest in developing our people and then they leave us?"
CEO: "What happens if we don't, and they stay?"
- Peter Baeklund

ATTRACTING, SELECTING, RETAINING, TRAINING AND COACHING OTHERS

The function of staffing is one of the most often overlooked of the six. Why? Because it takes time and energy to invest in selecting, training and growing people. This is typically not a natural favorite aspect of the job managers like or do well. As a manager you are unable to achieve goals without great people. Therefore, you are responsible – directly or indirectly – for development of staff, including proper and effective selection, appraisal and coaching. If you aren't successful in attracting, hiring and retaining great talent, the other functions suffer. It is hard to plan, organize and execute if you don't know if your staff will stay or conversely stay but not be a right fit for the position. Your team is the primary vehicle for accomplishing the goals of the business; without having the right people on board, with the appropriate skill set, passion, attitude and application to the job, your management effort rises and your overall effectiveness may suffer. We have all experienced the effects of a wrong hire over time. Many times managers hang onto the wrong personnel for too long, which can negatively impact the whole team, including themselves.

ASPECTS OF STAFFING:

- Retain key employees for long term staffing plans

- Develop all staff, including under-performing, aspiring, and high performing members

- Build a recruiting network and recruit pipeline — even when you are not hiring

- Invest time in coaching staff

- Provide training opportunities for technical and soft skills

- Evaluate your effectiveness with people

RECRUITING - THE FIRST STEP

There are many factors that can impact your ability to find high quality candidates for open job positions. These include: location of your business in regard to available labor pool, the state of the economy, pay, benefits and other companies in the area competing for similar talent. Don't let these obstacles deter you. The right person is always out there!

FILLING THE JOB

To identify whom you should be hiring for an open job, review, update and use the job role and key accountabilities as your starting point.

1 Are the job roles and key responsibilities clear?

2 How long has it been since the job position has been reviewed, and roles and key accountabilities updated?

3 Will the position be changing significantly over the next 12-24 months?

4 In addition to specific skills required for the position, what additional competencies would enhance the applicant's ability to be promoted?

5 Make sure that technical skills are separated from soft, behavioral skills required for the position.

6 Identify other aspects of the position important to consider/ discuss those which have not been outlined.

With thorough interviewing techniques, a candidate you initially thought was your least desired person can end up being your best hire.

COMMON INTERVIEWING PITFALLS

Consider the following when you move into hiring mode at your organization. Too often people interview applicants without knowing what to ask or how to ask questions.

PREPARATION - Going in prepared is important to conducting a successful interview. By doing this you will demonstrate:

- Clearly understanding the requirements, skills and behaviors needed for the position

- Being able to concisely communicate details about the role and related responsibilities
- Staying on course, not drifting into non job-related issues/tasks
- Being prepared not only makes sure you stay on track, but demonstrates how organized and professional you are as a manager

FIRST IMPRESSION – Although first impressions should be taken into account, they are not the only aspect of decision making when interviewing.

CONVERSATION – As an interviewer, you should never dominate the conversation:

- Careful listening is important as the applicant's personality, desires and areas of further development cannot be identified if you are doing all of the talking

STRESS – Be mindful that your applicants are likely to be feeling stress, and treat them kindly.

CONSISTENCY – Be consistent from one applicant to the next.

QUESTIONS – When asking questions, make sure that they remain relevant to the organization, and/or position.

HALO EFFECT – Don't overlook the candidate's overall ability because one trait or skill is outstanding.

HORN EFFECT – Conversely, don't assume that the one weak trait or skill is representative of all traits or skills.

HUNCH – Although having a 'hunch' or feeling in your 'gut' is fine, this shouldn't be the sole decision maker.

CONTROL – Having control over the interview doesn't mean you are not allowing the applicant to talk, but you want to ensure that the interview doesn't turn into the applicant interviewing you!

If you feel you are unwilling or unable to ask job-related questions of the candidate, get advice or coaching from an experienced person before taking on this task.

BEHAVIORAL INTERVIEWING QUESTIONS

Behavioral interviewing uses a questioning approach known as "Behavioral Analysis Questioning." These questions draw from the applicant's past behavior, and take the form of "Tell me about a time when...." In using Behavioral Analysis Questions (BAQ's) you always ask the applicant to tell you about something that he or she did previously relating to a skill, ability or experience that is needed for the job for which you are hiring. It has been shown that one of the best predictors of future behavior is past behavior. BAQ's can help indicate how they are likely to perform in the future.

BAQ's are very effective because they focus the interview on past behavior and NOT on opinions and views about oneself. They keep the interview on track, focusing on important job-related behaviors.

BEHAVIORAL ANALYSIS QUESTIONS (BAQ'S)

BAQ's are typically developed based on job-related critical incidents or success factors. Points to consider include:

- A critical incident is a situation in which an individual's performance will have significant consequences for the effective performance of a task

- They ask open-ended questions

- Using open-ended questions encourages the applicant to provide more details about their accomplishments and achievements. Use lead-ins like:

  - Describe for me a time when...

  - Tell me about when you performed that activity...

  - What can you tell me about...

  - They contain superlative adjectives - for example...

  - Ask for phrasing about the greatest extent or degree of something (most, best, hardest, most emotional, etc.) are essential to asking effective BAQ's.

- They are designed to, and should probe for additional information

- Each BAQ must have a series of follow-up questions designed to elicit more specific information about the incident or situation being described. These probing questions allow you to seek out exactly how the applicant behaved and what the consequences of that behavior were. Examples could include:

  - Take me through what you did, step by step

  - What led up to this situation?

  - What were the steps you used to carry that out?

  - Who was involved?

- What was the outcome?

- Once probing on each BAQ, ask yourself:

  - Do I have enough information so that I could describe this achievement/experience to someone else?

  - Do I know who, where, what, when and how related to the situation?

BEHAVIORAL ANALYSIS QUESTION

BAQ	Tell me about the most recent time that you went out of your way to help a fellow employee.
PROBING QUESTIONS	What was the situation? What specifically did you do? How did your co-worker respond? What was the result or the outcome?

Think about the BAQ question above and write down three additional questions in areas that would be important for you to know about the candidate:

SKILLS AND ATTRIBUTES

The following non-technical skills should be considered for each job position; use the relevant ones to evaluate each applicant during the interview process.

ADMINISTRATIVE SKILLS

Applicants with these skills demonstrate the ability to structure courses of action for self and others for efficient task completion, as well as the ability to use resources appropriately and to set priorities.

DECISION MAKING SKILLS

Applicants with these skills demonstrate the ability to make decisions based on a clear-cut, logical rationale that recognizes the implications for their own or others' components of the organization.

INITIATIVE/ENERGY SKILLS

Applicants with these skills demonstrate the ability to self-start and execute tasks without being told, and work in the interests of the organization, even if this means small personal sacrifices.

STRESS TOLERANCE SKILLS

Applicants with these skills demonstrate the ability to maintain performance and act with socially acceptable behavior when placed in a stressful situation.

HUMAN RELATIONS SKILLS

Applicants with these skills demonstrate the ability to work cooperatively with fellow workers, adapting their own behavior in order to work effectively with others.

LEADERSHIP SKILLS

Applicants with these skills demonstrate the ability to assume and perform a leadership role in the accomplishment of a task.

CUSTOMER SERVICE SKILLS

Applicants with these skills demonstrate the ability to consistently deliver and support superior customer service under a variety of unique and challenging circumstances. They also demonstrate the ability to provide customer service through their own action and by motivating, training and coaching others.

SEVEN STEP INTERVIEW PROCESS

The following seven-step process has been outlined to help you understand how the interview process should flow and how much time to focus on each section. This type of organized process will create consistency across all interviews.

STEP 1
1-2 MINUTES

- Arrange the physical environment for a comfortable and relaxing atmosphere
- Greet the applicant at the door
- Ask the applicant what he/she prefers to be called, and honor that preference
- If the applicant appears nervous, break the ice with 'small talk'
- Tell the applicant the purpose and structure of the interview

STEP 2
2-3 MINUTES

- Describe exactly what the applicant would be doing if he/she were hired
- Review the job description (if applicable)
- Ask if the applicant has any questions

STEP 3
3-5 MINUTES

- Verify that the applicant meets the minimum qualifications for employment: Salary and Physical
  Note: Sometimes this step is conducted prior to the face-to-face interview

STEP 4
10-20 MINUTES

- Ask questions about accomplishments and achievements related to the job requirements and responsibilities
- Ask follow up questions to gain more in-depth information

STEP 5
20-25 MINUTES

- Have applicant describe past work experiences related to the position
- Use BAQ's to determine how they contributed to the organization

STEP 6
5-10 MINUTES

- Use questions to determine if the applicant will be satisfied in the job, such as
  - What is it about this position that attracts you?
  - What do you see as positive aspects of this job? Negative aspects?

STEP 7
3-5 MINUTES

- Close the interview in a way that leaves a positive feeling about the company and the interview experience
- Ask questions like:
  - Is there anything else about you that is important for us to know?
  - What questions

THINGS TO KEEP IN MIND WHILE INTERVIEWING:

- Ask one question at a time

- Be consistent (do not significantly change questions from one applicant to the next)

- Use probing to gather information that is not offered in response to the main questions (avoid probes that the applicant has already addressed in his/her responses)

- Do not reveal your thinking (e.g., acting surprised or discouraged by an answer)

- Take notes on the applicant's behavioral answers

- Remind the applicant that you prefer job-related responses

- Stop the applicant with a closing question if they are spending too long on an answer

- Monitor the time and the progress you are making through the interview

- At the end of the interview, provide the applicant a chance to ask you questions or to add anything that they think is important

- Sincerely thank the applicant for coming and explain what will happen next

SAMPLE INTERVIEW EVALUATION FORM

APPLICANT NAME: _____   POSITION: _____

INTERVIEWER: _____   DATE: _____

Rate the applicant's overall level on each to the following **SKILLS** and **ABILITIES** using the 1 – 5 scale with 1 being low and 5 being high. Refer to your notes from the interview.

SKILLS	1	2	3	4	5
Administrative Skills					
Decision Making					
Initiative / Energy					
Stress Tolerance					
Human Relations Skills					
Leadership Skills					

Rate the applicant's overall level on each to the following **JOB FIT INDEX** using the 1 – 5 scale with 1 being low and 5 being high. Refer to your notes from the interview.

JOB FIT INDEX AREAS	1	2	3	4	5
Work Ethic					
Work Values					
Work Preferences					
Work Style					
Maturity					
Responsibility					
Teamwork					

"I absolutely believe that people, unless coached, never reach their maximum capabilities."
Bob Nardelli, former CEO, Home Depot

RETAINING AND DEVELOPING EMPLOYEES THROUGH COACHING

Once you have the right team in place, or you have gone through the interview and recruiting process successfully, your role as a manager is to provide continuous development for your team. This can be provided in a variety of ways, directly or indirectly. These include, but are not limited to:

- Directly training/coaching the team yourself

- Recommending other training opportunities

- Utilizing internal company training and development resources if they exist

- Using discretionary funds from a budget dedicated to individual development through external resources

PROVIDING OR DELIVERING STAFF COACHING

Coaching is a very specific developmental process by which an individual works with a coach to focus on developing key areas of performance for next level job satisfaction, productivity and motivation.

A key role of a manager is to help develop their staff through coaching. Yet very few managers have been provided education or training to be a professional skills coach. Many people have what I call "sports" based coaching skills. This coaching form is referred to as a "directive" based method. There is an alternative to directive coaching which is called "in-directive coaching".

While coaching has been utilized to correct performance issues, it is generally considered a developmental process. I developed my coaching skills by being coached, on the job application, reading and sharing techniques with other coaches. My favorite authored coaching source is Myles Downey, who wrote "Effective Coaching". The following overviews are derivatives of Myles' process.

DIRECTIVE COACHING – PUSH

THIS STYLE IS REPRESENTATIVE OF SOMEONE SOLVING ANOTHER'S PROBLEMS FOR THEM.

Providing instruction, direction, giving advice, providing answers, giving feedback and making suggestions to the person being coached.

As mentioned above, directive coaching is utilized in sports or athletic development. This style involves having the coach (manager) provide very specific, directive feedback to the person being coached on what they need to change, start doing, stop doing or continue doing. Whether it's football, basketball, tennis or gymnastics, directive coaching is designed to have the coach tell, sell and ensure the person receiving the coaching applies the directives until they become natural. This requires a lot of direct observation and in-the-moment feedback.

IN-DIRECTIVE COACHING – PULL

THIS STYLE IS REPRESENTATIVE OF SOMEONE HELPING ANOTHER SOLVE THEIR OWN PROBLEMS.

Listening to understand, reflecting, paraphrasing, summarizing and asking questions that raise awareness. Self-discovery and learning is the goal.

In-directive coaching is designed to have the coach assess another's situation and ask guiding questions with the goal of taking the other person to the next level through personal discovery. It involves a shift from telling to asking, from having the coach provide all the answers to having the person being coached discover them, in how learning occurs and development begins to take root. Active listening skills and good probing questions are key to be a successful coach in the process. When using the in-directive coaching model, a five step process exists that can be utilized to help the coach guide the person receiving coaching through the learning process and provide outcome-based sessions.

The process includes:

- **SELECTING A TOPIC**: Understand the coaching topic
- **GOAL**: Identify a coaching session goal
- **REALITY**: What, Who, Where and How factors
- **OPTIONS**: What options exist as possible solutions
- **WRAP-UP**: Select options, gain clarity, get a commitment, provide support

IN-DIRECTIVE COACHING QUESTIONS

Below are some sample questions to help you get started and stay on focus when providing in-directive coaching:

TOPIC EXAMPLES

- What would you like to discuss?
- What instruction would you like to focus on?

GOAL EXAMPLES

- What do you want to be different once our coaching sessions are complete?
- What is your goal or outcome for this session?

REALITY EXAMPLES

- Specifically, what is it you are having a challenge with?
- What have you done in the past to address this challenge?
- How did things turn out?

The indirective coaching process above is also referred to as the GROW model.

OPTIONS EXAMPLES

- Based on the way things are today, would a prior approach or solution work?
- What else is a possible option to help solve this challenge?

WRAP-UP EXAMPLES

- Out of all the options identified, which sounds most interesting/viable to you?

CLARITY | COMMITMENT EXAMPLES

- To clarify, you will implement this solution next week?

Follow up with restating the objective, goal and desire to support if needed.

A TRUE STORY

MAKING HIRING DECISIONS

I utilize the DISC instrument as part of my interviewing process and to profile an actual job position. I had a workshop administrator job open at one time and had identified a required job profile of compliance and steadiness as primary behavioral qualities, with dominance and influencing as low.

Having the behavioral profile of the job made it easier for me to map that to the candidates' actual behavioral profiles. I had all candidates applying for the job take the DISC assessment. I was using this report as only one-third of my decision making process, but a very important third it was. The DISC report has two graphs, an adapted and a natural, which graphically describe one's behaviors. This allows me to see people's behavioral makeup in the work environment and outside of work. If the graphs match or are very similar, then the persons behavior can be predicted to be the same inside work as it is outside. If the graphs are different, then it tells me this person is adapting their behavior to do the job. If their adapted graph changes significantly from their natural, it tells me the person may, could or will experience stress in doing the job, which is not good for long term job satisfaction. One candidate, Mary, had the perfect profile in her adapted or work environment graph. I got very excited as she matched the behavioral job profile perfectly! The job called for a high compliant, analytical person with a desire to have a steady predictable work environment. Then I glanced over to her natural style, and my heart sank...her natural graph was opposite the job. She was naturally a high Influencer, which told me she needed a lot of people contact! I said, "Mary, I would like to hire you, but I will tell you I believe you would be better off going into sales or marketing." She stared at me with wide eyes and said, "How did you know that?! I have been wanting to go into sales or marketing for years!" I replied, "It's all right here in your profile and report. You are a people person and need variety and creativity. I believe you could adapt and do this job as your work environment graph shows that, but I believe you would be unhappy over time."

I did not hire her, she went on her way with a renewed energy and focus as a result if the interview and I pursued someone who fit the job almost perfectly.

MORAL OF THE STORY: Don't hire people based on first impressions, gut instincts or on skills alone. People usually hire for skill and fire for bad behavior. Take your time and utilize hiring tools to ensure you make the best hire. You want to keep employees and invest in people that will make your life easy in the long run!

STAFFING SKILLS ASSESSMENT

The following assessment is designed to evaluate several of your Staffing skill areas. Other development points to consider include:

- Reviewing history on selecting, interviewing and coaching success

- Getting/asking for direct feedback from your staff and/or direct reports

- Getting feedback from upper management

- Fostering dialogue based development

1 I define job competencies:

1 POOR	☐	2 FAIR	☐	3 AVERAGE	☐	4 GOOD	☐	5 EXCELLENT	☐

2 I am effective in the interview process:

1 POOR	☐	2 FAIR	☐	3 AVERAGE	☐	4 GOOD	☐	5 EXCELLENT	☐

3 I provide training to my staff:

1 POOR	☐	2 FAIR	☐	3 AVERAGE	☐	4 GOOD	☐	5 EXCELLENT	☐

4 I invest time in coaching, mentoring and developing my team:

1 POOR	☐	2 FAIR	☐	3 AVERAGE	☐	4 GOOD	☐	5 EXCELLENT	☐

5 I facilitate development:

1 POOR	☐	2 FAIR	☐	3 AVERAGE	☐	4 GOOD	☐	5 EXCELLENT	☐

6 I encourage continuous learning:

1 POOR	☐	2 FAIR	☐	3 AVERAGE	☐	4 GOOD	☐	5 EXCELLENT	☐

7 I appraise performance consistently and effectively:

1 POOR	☐	2 FAIR	☐	3 AVERAGE	☐	4 GOOD	☐	5 EXCELLENT	☐

8 I resolve performance issues:

1 POOR	☐	2 FAIR	☐	3 AVERAGE	☐	4 GOOD	☐	5 EXCELLENT	☐

9 I recognize and reward good performance:

1 POOR	☐	2 FAIR	☐	3 AVERAGE	☐	4 GOOD	☐	5 EXCELLENT	☐

TOTAL AVERAGE SCORE:

Total all scores and divide by 9

Now that you have your scores, select the lowest and use the IGOAsm Worksheet for creating a Staffing focused goal and action plan.

ISSUE:

GOAL:

OBSTACLES: to attain my goal

ACTION PLAN: focused in overcoming my top 3 obstacles, which will get me to my goal

ACTION ITEM	WHO	WHEN

"People are typically hired for their skills and terminated for their behavior."

- Unknown

FUNCTION FIVE

CONTROLLING

"Inspect what you expect"
- Brian Tracy

MONITORING RESULTS, COMPARING TO PLAN & TAKING CORRECTIVE ACTION

The word "controlling" seems uncomfortable to many managers at first, because of the negative connotation that it can have. Terminology aside, it can also be a positive aspect of management; the function of controlling verifies whether performance meets required standards. Control is an important feature of measurement and measuring results regularly is a way to ensure you execute to plan.

Consider sailing as an analogy to function of controlling: when sailing a boat, constant corrective action is necessary to guarantee that it gets to the destination. There are many variables that can easily throw you off course – water conditions, current, wind, equipment, obstacles in the water, etc. A sailboat captain must make constant adjustments – pulling in the sail, turning the helm, putting up the jib – to make sure the boat hits its mark.

Think of managing your work plans as akin to captaining a sailboat and you will see that the controlling function helps ensure you land where you want to be.

ASPECTS OF CONTROLLING:

- Communicate goals and expectations clearly

- Ensure monitoring process and standards are explained

- Build consensus around team meeting process and protocol

- Instill self-accountability and a corrective action process

- Be open to innovation for performance improvements

FUNCTIONS OF CONTROLLING

Managers may confuse controlling with micromanaging, or needing to be heavily involved in gaining results. Definition of the term is designed to look back at the goals and objectives set out in Planning and use those as milestones for measurement. Essentially, this function is about 'inspecting what you expect'. Many managers struggle with this and how to best utilize team meetings to harness discussion about goals and results. Without clear goals or targets, regular inspection of progress, and accountable corrective action, the wind may take you and your team elsewhere!

CONTROLLING AT A HIGH LEVEL IS:

CLEARLY COMMUNICATING GOALS	▪ Establishing a vision ▪ Ensure team members understand goals and are committed to them
ESTABLISHING STANDARDS OF PERFORMANCE	▪ Communicate standards ▪ Adhere to standards
MEASURING AND EVALUATING RESULTS	▪ Use team meetings to communicate, coordinate, and review progress toward goals ▪ Obtain timely reports ▪ Compare margin information vs. cost ▪ 80% of the information is in 20% of the data ▪ Control by both exceptions and personal inspection ▪ Have individual team member meetings (1x1's)
TAKING ACTION REGARDING PERFORMANCE	▪ Goal achieved: reward performance ▪ Goal not achieved: review corrective action plan or modify goal ▪ Follow up

GOALS VS. OPERATIONS

Goals have a very specific purpose for businesses, including, but not limited to:

- Ensuring growth, profitability and market share targets are attained

- Providing a common focal point or vision for company direction

- Providing milestones by which efforts are measured

With this in mind, a focus on goals helps an organization sustain growth in future years.

Operations keep the business moving each day. Managers spend most of their time and energy in this area as day-to-day issues and projects demand it.

That said, goals are key to business growth and operations have an important role in maintaining that growth. This is where the Kerr Hill philosophy of "Operations keep us in business today" and "Goals keep us in business tomorrow" comes from.

TEAM MEETINGS

Team meetings should result in measurable outcomes. Many, if not most, managers despise meetings, or at least the number of meetings they are required to attend. Why? Because most meetings are not managed properly, resulting in wasted time. When you host a one hour meeting with eight people attending, it is not a one hour meeting, it is an eight hour meeting, meaning eight hours of valuable resources are being tied up. Therefore running efficient, effective meetings is crucial.

A TYPICAL MEETING

The typical team meeting has some sort of agenda, with topics for discussion. Team members assemble and begin discussing 'operations-based issues' and tasks. Discussion tends to stray to new operational issues as a result of the initial topic. Before you know it, an hour has passed and a whole lot of dialogue, ideas and opinion-sharing have gone on. More than likely, it has run over the allotted time. Adjourning, what do the team members leave with? Maybe some clarity on team goals but most times not enough to make their time invested of value. The next meeting picks up on the topics from the last meeting and thus begins a never-ending cycle of meetings.

There are exceptions and there are managers who run effective team meetings, but corporate America generally does not have this issue under control.

When you host a one hour meeting with eight people, it is not a one hour meeting, it is an eight hour meeting.

OPERATIONS KEEP US IN BUSINESS TODAY

GOALS KEEP US IN BUSINESS TOMORROW!

THE MANAGEMENT TEAM MEETING PROCESS

The Management Team Meeting (MTMsм) process was specifically designed to help managers keep their teams and meetings focused on goals and goal progress. This includes having teams create and report on progress towards monthly goals, with self-accountable corrective actions when goals are not being met.

ISSUES MATRIX	VITAL ISSUES	NON-VITAL ISSUES
URGENT ISSUES	OPERATIONS	
NON-URGENT ISSUES	GOALS	

Most managers and their teams focus on operational issues with the bulk of their time. After all, that is what they are here to do: help, support and keep operations running. Where does discussion and review of strategic goals live? While existing on paper as part of a plan, goal based dialogue takes a back seat when it comes to focused discussion in team meetings. The matrix above provides an example of where operations and goals live and where managers spend most of their time. Operational issues often fill the vital and urgent categories. Goals, meanwhile, usually live down below in the non-urgent box even though they are vital to growth and survival of the business. Since goals "keep us in business tomorrow", I recommend managers invert the location of each, placing goals in the Vital and Urgent box. Easy to say, harder to do...but with the MTM$_{SM}$ process, it can be accomplished very effectively. So where do discussions about operational issues happen? In a separate meeting focused on Operational issues! If you want to get a great perspective on meetings management, read Patrick Lencioni's "Death by Meeting".

WHERE AND HOW TO BEGIN FOCUSING MORE ON GOALS?

The MTM$_{SM}$ process begins with creating crisp, clear, 30-day business goals focused on the top issues facing the business. As described in the chapter on Planning, the goals created there come into play with the process.

IMPLEMENTING MTM$_{SM}$ AS YOUR PRIMARY BUSINESS MEETING DEVICE

The Goal of MTM$_{SM}$ is to clearly understand progress towards goals and identify corrective actions in getting to those goals. The approach to utilizing and implementing the MTM$_{SM}$ process follows.

WEEK 1

FILL OUT GOAL PROGRESS REPORT WITH TEAM

- Communicate monthly team goals
- Have team members fill out their forms and goals for the month
- Review goals, discuss, approve, make copies
- Adjourn

WEEK 2

CAPTURE GOAL PROGRESS WITH TEAM

- Have team members report on goal progress in first week
- Collect results, acknowledge success or ask for corrective action if goals in first week were missed
- Transfer all corrective actions to the team meeting minutes page
- Adjourn

WEEK 3

CAPTURE GOAL PROGRESS WITH TEAM

- Have team members report on goal progress in second week
- Collect results, acknowledge success or ask for corrective action
- Transfer all corrective actions to the team meeting minutes page
- Adjourn

CAPTURE GOAL PROGRESS, COMPLETE MONTH FORM

WEEK 4

- Have team members report on goal progress in third week
- Qualify, collect results, acknowledge success or ask for corrective action
- Transfer all corrective actions to the team meeting minutes page
- Acknowledge results and begin process for the next month with a new Goal Progress Reporting form
- Adjourn

The Management Team Meeting (MTMsm) process is your primary control device designed to focus you and your team on goal versus operational based team meetings.

CONTROLLING AND MONITORING – STAYING FOCUSED

The Goal Progress Report system provides a way to review progress towards goals in an effective, simple manner. Operational issues are typically not discussed during this process. The following is a blank and filled out sample of a Goal Progress Report Form.

NAME: [   ]   DEPARTMENT: [   ]   FROM: [   ]   TO: [   ]

GOALS	RESULTS	ACTION REQUIRED

SAMPLE GOAL PROGRESS REPORT

NAME: Bob Sample   Data Entry   [   ] [   ]

GOALS	RESULTS	ACTION REQUIRED
To reduce data entry errors	6/8/14 – Have not started.	6/8/14 – Need to meet with group to
To increase team productivity by 10% over the next thirty	6/8/14 – Met and discussed. Everyone has personal action...	6/8/14 – On Track
To reduce operation costs by 5% by	6/8/14 – Found several areas with...	6/8/14 – On Track

This sample Goal Progress Report shows goals for the month with the first week results reported. Corrective action items are noted on goals that are behind schedule.

NAME: Bob Sample   Data Entry

GOALS	RESULTS	ACTION REQUIRED
To reduce data entry errors	6/8/14 – Have not started.	6/8/14 – Need to meet with group to set vision
To increase team productivity by 10% over the next thirty days, or by 6/30/14	6/8/14 – Met and discussed. Everyone has personal action item(s) to bring to next	6/8/14 – On Track
To reduce operation costs by 5% by 6/30/14	6/8/14 – Found several areas with team, ahead	6/8/14 – On Track

Any corrective action items from the Goal Progress Report get written onto the meeting minutes form below. This consolidates all action items from the team for each session.

SAMPLE MANAGEMENT TEAM MEETING MINUTES FORM

MEETING CALLED BY:		MEETING DATE:	
ATTENDEES		NEXT MEETING:	

NO.	ACTION ITEM	PERSON RESPONSIBLE	DUE DATE
1	Need to meet with group to set vision and goal	Bob	6/8/14
2			
3			
4			
5			
6			
7			

PURPOSE OF THE MANAGEMENT TEAM MEETING

- To review progress toward goals consistently with focus

- To recognize personal and team accomplishments

- To set new goals that align with current business needs

- To develop corrective actions when goals are not being met

- To create team-based communications

- To stay focused on goals

IDENTIFY TEAM MEMBERS

- Utilize with remote or cross functional team members

- Understand roles related to goals

ANTICIPATING OBSTACLES

- Lack of an agenda or not following it

- Lack of performance measures

- Discussing operations problems

- Reviewing too much data

- Poor attendance

- Not enough data

A TRUE STORY

I HAVE NEVER HAD TO FIRE ANYONE

I believe in utilizing the tools I teach our clients to use, and I have employed the MTM_{SM} (Management Team Meeting Process) in my business for years. It has been highly effective for ensuring the organization is in alignment and all team members create and keep their commitments to goal-oriented actions.

Some years ago, I had an account manager named Todd, who had been with the company 2 months. At the weekly sales meetings, he regularly failed to meet the targets he had committed to the prior week. So every week he would say his corrective action was to make more phone calls and schedule more meetings, and each week when group reporting time came, he would have failed to meet his corrective actions. One week after a sales meeting, my top performing account manager came to me and said, "George, this sales meeting is becoming very de-motivating for me. I work hard and commit to my actions to meet company goals. Todd always gets to show up and keep his job even though he says he will do all the right things but fails to do so week after week. How is it a low performer gets to sit in the room with all of us top performers? That is not fair." I said, "Linda, you are right, it is not fair. I can see how it is a de-motivator. I will discuss this with him after this week's meeting."

Our meeting day came, and as usual, Todd reported that he had not done what he had committed to. As the meeting ended I was planning to ask him for a private conversation, but he actually approached me, saying, "George do you have moment?" I invited him into my office, and he proceeded to tell me that he felt bad that he could not fulfill the requirements of the job and was resigning from the company. I accepted his resignation and we parted ways amicably. I was going to terminate him, but he did me a favor and let himself go!

MORAL OF THE STORY: What I learned from this experience was two things; 1) inspect what you expect and 2) hold people accountable to their commitments. Don't wait too long to address performance issues. One single under-performer can de-motivate other team members. I believe the peer pressure was too much for Todd and as a result he left on his own. Had I not had this accountability process in place, Todd may have been there for many more months.

CONTROLLING SKILLS ASSESSMENT

The following points are designed to help evaluate your Controlling skills.

- Team meetings – are they focused on clear goals, results and action commitments?

- Are you meeting or exceeding goals set out in the planning phase? If no, why not?

- Do you demonstrate innovation through brainstorming and do things differently to get new results?

- Are you focusing too much time on operational issues?

1 I measure and evaluate results:

1 POOR		2 FAIR		3 AVERAGE		4 GOOD		5 EXCELLENT	

2 I gather performance data effectively:

1 POOR		2 FAIR		3 AVERAGE		4 GOOD		5 EXCELLENT	

3 I meet regularly with individual team members for review:

1 POOR		2 FAIR		3 AVERAGE		4 GOOD		5 EXCELLENT	

4 I discuss corrective actions required:

1 POOR		2 FAIR		3 AVERAGE		4 GOOD		5 EXCELLENT	

5 I follow through to completion:

1 POOR		2 FAIR		3 AVERAGE		4 GOOD		5 EXCELLENT	

6 I reinforce positive performance:

1 POOR		2 FAIR		3 AVERAGE		4 GOOD		5 EXCELLENT	

7 I encourage and practice self-control:

1 POOR		2 FAIR		3 AVERAGE		4 GOOD		5 EXCELLENT	

8 I facilitate continuous improvement:

1 POOR		2 FAIR		3 AVERAGE		4 GOOD		5 EXCELLENT	

TOTAL AVERAGE SCORE:

Total all scores and divide by 8

Now that you have your scores, select the lowest and use the IGOA_{SM} worksheet for creating your Controlling focused goal and action plan.

ISSUE:

GOAL:

OBSTACLES: to attain my goal

_____   _____

_____   _____

_____   _____

_____   _____

ACTION PLAN: focused in overcoming my top 3 obstacles, which will get me to my goal

ACTION ITEM	WHO	WHEN

"Measuring and acknowledging team progress towards goals creates accountability and results."

FUNCTION SIX
LEADING

CREATING INDIVIDUAL AND TEAM MOTIVATION TO ACHIEVE GOALS

"Setting an example is not the main means of influencing others; it is the only means." – *Einstein*

Leading is the process by which managers instruct, guide and oversee the performance of others to achieve predetermined goals. Related functional skills include influencing, inspiring, building teamwork and mentoring others towards the accomplishment of organizational goals.

There are so many diverse perspectives on leadership in the workplace that it can often be challenging to choose one guiding principle from the ones available. If you have read, listened to audio books, attended seminars, or been led or coached by a great a leader, you have a great foundation for shaping your leadership style.

I have learned through observing and modeling a variety of leadership attributes and kept what worked for me. As long as a trait resonates with who you are – your style, values, beliefs – then it is something to consider applying. I like to tell people that leadership is something they can learn, but should be uniquely theirs, their style and application. The good news is there are great frameworks and philosophies from which to mix and match.

Ultimately you need to look at your work environment, what you have been tasked to do as a leader, evaluate your team and their needs and then point the way!

An exercise I like to do in my workshops includes observing a video called Everest. This is a story about the first blind man to climb to the top of Mt. Everest. He did not do it alone, but with a select group of people he trusted and had climbed with before. There were a multitude of success factors that he and his team practiced along the journey which cumulatively helped ensure their success. When I ask people what they observed and believe are the key characteristics of successful leaders and teams, they consistently come up with the following list of attributes.

- **HIGH LEVEL COMMUNICATION** - consistent, open, adaptive

- **APPROACHABILITY** - with leader and all team members

- **DECISIVENESS** - the leader and team were very decisive

- **FLEXIBILITY** - they adapted quickly to obstacles

- **VISIONARY** - keeping the vision of success in their mind's eye

- **HUMILITY** - they were not afraid to admit mistakes or fears

- **FOCUS** - they never took their eye off the goal

- **AVAILABILITY** - everyone had access to the leader and team

- **CLARITY** - they all had the same goal/common purpose

- **TRUSTWORTHINESS** - they all trusted each other

- **EMPOWERMENT** - they were all empowered to help

"Leading is not something you do to people, it's something you do with them."
- Ken Blanchard, The Leadership Pill

EXERCISE Below, list the top 5 key leadership traits or characteristics you feel you need to have for your organization and team. This can also be an exercise you do WITH your team. Either way, sharing these traits and having discussion and even commitments to modeling them is one sure way to instigate and embed these into your culture.

ASPECTS OF LEADING

- Setting and communicating Vision, Mission and Goals

- Spending time strategizing

- Team building and team development

- Decision-making and decisiveness

- Problem solving – tackling problems that were not anticipated

THREE ASPECTS OF LEADERSHIP TO CONSIDER:

DEVELOP SELF-CONFIDENCE

- Assess your attributes
- Recognize and build on strengths
- Acquire more knowledge
- Develop positive character traits
- Sharpen judgment through evaluation of experience
- Consider the 'bigger picture' point of view

TAKE THE LEADER POSITION

- Take charge
- Point the way
- Demonstrate decisiveness
- Set an example
- Find new, better ways
- Create a climate for self-motivation

BUILD A TEAM

- Be available – listen, hear
- Permit give and take, encourage constructive opposition
- Involve team in goal setting
- Be aware of your team members as people

"One who thinks they lead, but has no followers, is only talking a walk."

MANAGING VS. LEADING

When does a manager need to manage and when does a manager need to lead? It depends! Having awareness is a key component of any developmental process. What opportunities do you have every day to manifest new leading skills? One way to acknowledge and assess your manager vs. leader traits is to review the model below. This is a simple comparison matrix of the differences between managing and leading provided by the MindTree™ group. Think about each contrasting point and associate each with an aspect of your daily routine. When should you leave your manager's hat on? When should you shift into leadership mode? There are no rules, so you get to decide. Change only happens when you can catch yourself in those moments to try a different approach. If you want to really get strategic, think about opportunities/situations before they arrive, and how you might model and approach them in a new mode. I believe great leaders put a lot of thought into how they want show up for certain situations. Consider using your Power Hour for this!

LEADERS		MANAGERS
CREATE NEW ORDER	—	MAINTAIN EXISTING ORDER
DEFINE RISKS	—	DE-RISK
OPPORTUNITY FOCUSED	—	RESOURCE FOCUSED
HAVE COMFORT IN AMBIGUITY	—	HAVE COMFORT IN CLARITY
ARE OPPORTUNITY CENTRIC	—	ARE CONSTRAINT CENTRIC
ARE BIG PICTURE ORIENTED	—	ARE DETAILED ORIENTED
ARE INNOVATIVE	—	ARE ADAPTIVE

DECISION MAKING

The simplest thing you can do to understand what someone's motivators are is to ask.

Decision making is highlighted in this function because it is an important part of leading and managing. Leaders cannot maintain success long if they have a track record of bad decision making. Your manager and team look to you for direction, decisiveness and confidence. People like to follow decisive leaders, even if at times they make an incorrect decision. Good leaders can make decisions fairly quickly and without frequently changing their minds. Slow decision making with regular changes does not provide a leader or their team with the confidence they need to move forward.

If we could look into the future to see what outcomes we could have with the decisions we make today, life would be grand. Since it doesn't work that way, you need to rely on past experience, current information, some intuition or gut hunch and ability to assess risk. Great leaders get over possibly having made a wrong decision quickly.

DECISION MAKING FACTORS

Consider the following factors when making decisions:

CLARITY ON ISSUES AT HAND – Is the issue you are trying to make a decision on clear to you?

RELEVANT INFORMATION – Do you have all the relevant information you need in the moment to evaluate all sides? Are you waiting too long for more information to show up?

CONSTRAINTS – Have you evaluated all the current constraints and obstacles? These may include, but are not limited to, time, money, team ability, culture, systems, tools, technology, and clear communication.

RISK – Have you looked at risk level on your decisions? For example, on a scale of 1-5, 1 being very low risk and 5 being high

– what impact will your decisions have on you, your team and the organization if you move forward with them? Are you naturally a high risk-taker, or too conservative too often? If so, what can you do to balance out either extreme?

RESOURCES – Most business decisions are influenced by resources or lack thereof. The three primary resources most managers have to work with are: time, money and assets like people, tools, equipment or vendors. If you had unlimited availability to all three of these resources, your decisions might be quick and easy most of the time! Reality says you don't have unlimited availability to all three of these, so you must decide what you can commit to accomplishing given time, people and budget at hand.

MOTIVATING YOURSELF AND TEAM MEMBERS

TOP TEN EMPLOYEE MOTIVATORS

Understanding, supporting and maintaining team motivation is key for all managers, including you! You must know your own motivators and de-motivators, so you can model the kind of behavior you would like from your team and peers. You set the tone for your team every time you walk through the door. If you understand your motivators and share those with your manager for ongoing support, the likelihood is that your motivation will sustain itself.

The next level of motivation has to do with your team or peers. A highly motivated team can increase productivity and results beyond what you thought possible. It is a known fact that highly motivated people and teams deliver more creative, effective results. There are basically two ways to understand people's motivators. One is to observe their actions and the other is to ask.

Managers have a tendency to either forget, not care, or assume they know what people's motivators are.

Often employees think differently than their managers. Results from employee satisfaction surveys below show the difference between what managers believe employees want versus employees. Managers often believe that MONEY is a primary job motivator, while employees say they want APPRECIATION more than anything else.

EMPLOYEES WANT	MANAGERS THINK THEY WANT
Appreciation	Good Wages
Feeling 'in' on things	Job Security
Understanding	Promotion Opportunities
Job Security	Good Working Conditions
Good Wages	Interesting Work
Interesting Work	Loyalty from Management
Promotion Opportunities	Tactful Discipline
Loyalty from Management	Appreciation
Good Working Conditions	Understanding
Tactful Discipline	Feeling 'in' on things

EXERCISE

Take a moment to think about and write down the top three things that motivate you to do the job you do. When done, do the same with the de-motivators below.

TOP 3 WORKPLACE MOTIVATORS

1.

2.

3.

TOP 3 WORKPLACE DE-MOTIVATORS

1.

2.

3.

WHAT MOTIVATES YOUR STAFF?

Your job as a leader is to keep your team motivated, not to fill their daily motivational gas tank. This means people need to show up with a fair amount of personal motivation for you to sustain and grow.

The motivators, de-motivators exercise is simple and easy to perform with your team or peers, in a group or individual setting. Group sessions allow for a greater level of dialogue and sharing of motivators, not only for you, but for everyone on the team. If you decide to conduct it in a group setting, prepare everyone by explaining the logic of the exercise. For example, you might say, "One of my key responsibilities and focus as your leader is to see us all succeed. One way to accomplish that is to ensure that we all stay motivated. When you look forward to work and enjoy what you do, it enhances your life. If I better understand the top three things that keep you motivated, and those that de-motivate you, it will allow me to support motivational needs and eliminate de-motivators on an ongoing basis." Once you know what people's motivators/de-motivators are, the next question is to ask if they are getting their motivators supported.

I have personally witnessed some very profound conversations when facilitating this exercise for participants from my program with their managers. Managers always want to know how to better motivate their people. Some people can be motivated, others can't. Motivation lives within each of us on an intrinsic level, meaning there are things that satisfy us internally, personally. There are also extrinsic motivators that can motivate us such as money, objects, titles, etc. Everyone has their own motivational balance if you will. As a manager your job is to understand people's motivators and do as much as you can to fuel them.

TEAMWORK

The essence of effective team leadership is measured by how well your team interacts, communicates and rallies to support your vision, direction and initiatives. Without solid teamwork, individual efforts to move the business in the right direction may be limited or wasted.

Your personal and professional success will depend on your ability to build and lead a great team.

When I poll people in my workshops by asking how many take time with their teams to specifically discuss teamwork, I am always amazed to find no one raises their hand. Most team leaders and teams do not invest time in reviewing, exploring, discussing or creating teamwork based conversation, guidelines or rules of engagement! So how and where do you begin? Most people promoted into leadership roles have experience in business, know the technical aspects of their job and have been on or led teams on some level. They would not have been promoted if they didn't have signs of leadership and the ability to lead others. Most have a pretty good idea of what they need to do to get everyone on the same page, from a technical delivery standpoint. Many have a hard time knowing where to begin discussing teamwork as a topic with their team. One starting point is to read or listen to a book. You can attend a team building seminar or bring a specialist in that does team development. You can scour the Internet and get a wide perspective on all the models and approaches available. The number of resources is virtually unlimited. It is more important to educate and apply, than to do nothing and hope that teamwork will naturally happen. Application is different than theory. It can be more difficult, but is well worth the effort. I have seen many team leaders stretch, apply and succeed as a result. Here are some initial questions to ask yourself as you build and support teamwork. Are you inheriting a team that has been around for a long time? If so, do they have long term habits and dynamics that other leaders have tried to change and failed? Are their motivators to succeed high or low? Alternatively, do you have the ability to select and build a new team? What will be the most important qualities in the team members you will be looking to add? Is technical know-how more important than attitude and behavior, or desire to be the best? Are there some team members that are not a good fit for the team? Are they consistently negative and create conflict with you and others? Do you have a clear picture in your mind about how you would like to see the team functioning that you can clearly communicate?

One of the best and most common team-building methodologies on the market is The Five Dysfunctions of a Team framework. Author Patrick Lencioni does a wonderful job constructing his learning points through business fables. This story is about a new CEO coming into a high tech business to turn the dysfunctional senior management team around. She uses the Five Dysfunctions model to eventually create a high performance team through Patrick's five step process. Aside from the book, there is a field guide and a comprehensive on-line assessment tool that helps you assess your teamwork levels. I have worked with many teams utilizing and implementing Patrick's model and the techniques work very successfully.

THE FIVE DYSFUNCTIONS OF A TEAM DEFINED

Below is a brief overview of each dysfunction. A team may be strong in four areas and weak in one or vice versa. The idea behind having a fully functioning high powered team is to be strong in all five areas.

TRUST – Unwillingness to be vulnerable within the group. Team members who are not genuinely open with each other about their weaknesses and mistakes make it impossible to build a foundation of trust.

FEAR OF CONFLICT – Teams that lack trust are incapable of engaging in unfiltered and passionate debate of ideas. Instead they resort to veiled discussions and guarded comments.

LACK OF COMMITMENT – Without having aired their opinions in the course of open passionate debate, team members rarely, if ever, buy in and commit to decisions, though they say they do during meetings.

AVOIDANCE OF ACCOUNTABILITY – Without committing to a clear plan of action, even the most focused and driven people often hesitate to call their peers on actions and behaviors that seem counterproductive to the good of the team.

INATTENTION TO RESULTS – This occurs when team members place their individual needs (ego, career, development or recognition) or even the needs of their divisions above the collective goals of the team.

If you do not know how to evaluate your current situation with regard to the Five Dysfunctions model and are you interested in finding out, follow the link below to inquire about this assessment:

🔗 http://www.thesixfunctions.com/fiveds

A TRUE STORY
A PERSPECTIVE ON LEADERSHIP

I once went to a motivational seminar for the industry I was working in, and the presenter was a very dynamic, funny professional. He asked the audience if anyone had ever been bitten by an elephant. I looked around the room and not one person put their hand up. He then asked how many people had been bitten by a mosquito. Almost everyone's hands went up. What was his point? He said: "It's the little things in life that bite us!" This is so true. And in my experience it's the little things that matter most to the people on your team.

This really came home to me one day when I was talking with my office administrator. I don't recall what we were discussing, but out of nowhere she said: "You know George, you don't smile enough in here!" I said, "Yes I do!" She said, "No you don't." And I said, "Yes I do!" We could have gone a few more rounds, but I realized that she was right. I said, "Well, I do say good morning to everyone when I come in." She agreed, "Yes you do, but you don't smile." Nothing more needed to be said; it dawned on me that how I was showing up every day was setting the tone for my team and the office.

I went to my desk and tried to picture myself walking in every day. I had not done self-reflection like this before, but had to trust that if one of my employees was observing this it must be true. I could see what she was saying...as I walked in each day, I was focused on my list of things to do and what needed to be accomplished. I did not recall feeling a smile break on my face.

I was grateful she had the guts to give me unsolicited feedback. Had I not gotten this I would have continued with the same daily routine. It's the little things that matter to people!

There are many aspects to leadership that can impact your success, relationships with employees and clients. Self-awareness and desire to improve are two of the greatest traits one can have in developing their leadership skills.

All the traditional aspects of leadership are very important, things like effective communication, being approachable, ability to make good and timely decisions, being trusted and trustworthy, having integrity, developing others, building strong teams, creating vision, taking charge, etc. Great leaders also know when to step back and let their teams do their thing!

MORAL OF THE STORY: You set the tone for your employees every day. They look to you as their leader. Changing team tone can be as simple as smiling more often. In many ways you are responsible for them, for their daily experience and success. This is the responsibility leadership roles carry.

LEADING SKILLS ASSESSMENT

Consider the following points as options for evaluating your Leading skills.

- Obtain feedback through an organizational 360 feedback survey
- Ask your team and/or peers directly about your leadership style and impact
- Assess individual and team performance – are they doing well as a result of your leadership?

DECISION MAKING
SELECTING THE BEST SOLUTION

1 I analyze issues and information:

1 POOR	2 FAIR	3 AVERAGE	4 GOOD	5 EXCELLENT
☐	☐	☐	☐	☐

2 I maintain objectivity:

1 POOR	2 FAIR	3 AVERAGE	4 GOOD	5 EXCELLENT
☐	☐	☐	☐	☐

3 I am open to others' input:

1 POOR	2 FAIR	3 AVERAGE	4 GOOD	5 EXCELLENT
☐	☐	☐	☐	☐

4 I make decisions in a timely manner:

1 POOR	2 FAIR	3 AVERAGE	4 GOOD	5 EXCELLENT
☐	☐	☐	☐	☐

TEAMWORK
WORKING TOGETHER TO ACHIEVE A COMMON GOAL

1 I demonstrate willingness to be a team member:

1 POOR	2 FAIR	3 AVERAGE	4 GOOD	5 EXCELLENT
☐	☐	☐	☐	☐

2 I commit to team goals:

1 POOR	2 FAIR	3 AVERAGE	4 GOOD	5 EXCELLENT
☐	☐	☐	☐	☐

3 I give support to other teams' goals:

1 POOR	2 FAIR	3 AVERAGE	4 GOOD	5 EXCELLENT
☐	☐	☐	☐	☐

4 I coordinate with others to achieve goals:

1 POOR	2 FAIR	3 AVERAGE	4 GOOD	5 EXCELLENT
☐	☐	☐	☐	☐

5 I support team processes:

1 POOR	2 FAIR	3 AVERAGE	4 GOOD	5 EXCELLENT
☐	☐	☐	☐	☐

**LEADERSHIP
CREATING INDIVIDUAL
AND TEAM MOTIVATION**

1 I demonstrate self-confidence:

1 POOR	2 FAIR	3 AVERAGE	4 GOOD	5 EXCELLENT

2 I take charge and initiate action:

1 POOR	2 FAIR	3 AVERAGE	4 GOOD	5 EXCELLENT

3 I create enthusiasm for vision and direction:

1 POOR	2 FAIR	3 AVERAGE	4 GOOD	5 EXCELLENT

4 I empower others to act:

1 POOR	2 FAIR	3 AVERAGE	4 GOOD	5 EXCELLENT

5 I demonstrate decisiveness:

1 POOR	2 FAIR	3 AVERAGE	4 GOOD	5 EXCELLENT

6 I model leader competencies:

1 POOR	2 FAIR	3 AVERAGE	4 GOOD	5 EXCELLENT

7 I accept input on finding better ways:

1 POOR	2 FAIR	3 AVERAGE	4 GOOD	5 EXCELLENT

8 I creating a climate for motivation:

1 POOR	2 FAIR	3 AVERAGE	4 GOOD	5 EXCELLENT

9 I accept risk:

1 POOR	2 FAIR	3 AVERAGE	4 GOOD	5 EXCELLENT

10 I generate enthusiasm:

1 POOR	2 FAIR	3 AVERAGE	4 GOOD	5 EXCELLENT

11 I encourage and facilitate teamwork:

1 POOR	2 FAIR	3 AVERAGE	4 GOOD	5 EXCELLENT

12 I understand people:

1 POOR	2 FAIR	3 AVERAGE	4 GOOD	5 EXCELLENT

TOTAL AVERAGE SCORE:

Total all scores and divide by 22

Select your lowest score from the assessments on pages 136-137 and use the IGOA℠ Worksheet for creating a Leading focused goal and action plan.

ISSUE:

GOAL:

OBSTACLES: to attain my goal

_____   _____

_____   _____

_____   _____

_____   _____

ACTION PLAN: focused in overcoming my top 3 obstacles, which will get me to my goal

ACTION ITEM	WHO	WHEN

"Individual commitment to a group effort - that is what makes a team work, a company work, a society work, a civilization work."

- Vince Lombardi

IN CLOSING

Business management is hard work, whether you work for a large company, own a small business, or are an individual business contributor.

There are many aspects of managing a business that need to be considered and addressed. All people in management positions have strengths and weaknesses across the Six Functions.

Knowledge is power they say, and a clear understanding of your strengths and areas for improvement gives you the power to change your career on a day-to-day basis.

This planning guide was designed to provide you with an overview of how the Six Functions individually and collectively work together to provide a framework with which you can develop your management skills.

Awareness is one of the most powerful, empowering aspects of professional development. Without awareness, you don't know what you need to change or how your style impacts others around you. Self-assessment is a great starting point for personal and professional development, and is the foundation of this planning guide. I strongly advocate getting feedback from your team, organization or partners to cross check your personal perceptions. Most people can make a fairly accurate self-assessment, so there is no right or wrong, just verification and validation.

I have found the most successful personal development approaches have self-accountability and follow up built in. An accountability partner can be an immeasurable help in achieving your goals.

My aim with this planning guide has been to compile what is normally a three day learning experience and transform it into a self-guided process.

The Six Functions framework, tools, methods, systems within are time-tested principles, and I have seen firsthand what they have done for thousands of professionals worldwide.

I hope your personal and professional development journey is enjoyable and successful as a result.

GEORGE PHIRIPPIDIS

REFERENCES

ASSESSMENTS AVAILABLE THROUGH KERR HILL AT:

WWW.KERRHILL.COM/CONTACT

- DISC Behaviors, Motivators, Skills, Acumen, Emotional Intelligence

- The Thomas-Kilmann Instrument and the Five Modes of Conflict

- The 5 Dysfunctions of a Team Assessment

- Kerr Hill 360 Feedback Reports - Leader and Manager, Custom

PROGRAM INFORMATION

- **Managers Performance Program:**
  http://www.kerrhill.com/programs-managers

- **Supervisors Development Program:**
  http://www.kerrhill.com/programs-supervisors

- **Executive Development Program:**
  http://www.kerrhill.com/programs-executive

- **A list of all Kerr Hill Programs:**
  http://www.kerrhill.com/programs-line-card

BOOKS AND RECOMMENDED READINGS

- Jim Collins - Good to Great

- Ken Blanchard - The Leadership Pill

- Kerry Patterson - Crucial Conversations

- Michael Gerber - The E-Myth

- Myles Downey - Effective Coaching

- Patrick Lencioni - Death By Meeting, The Five Dysfunctions of a Team, Getting Naked, The Advantage

- Roger Fisher, William Ury - Getting to Yes

- Stephen Covey - The Seven Habits of Highly Effective People

72299146R00082